2-D Geometry

Sunken Ships and Grid Patterns

Grade 4

Also appropriate for Grade 5

Douglas H. Clements
Michael T. Battista
Joan Akers
Andee Rubin
Virginia Woolley

Developed at TERC, Cambridge, Massachusetts

Dale Seymour Publications®
Menlo Park, California

The *Investigations* curriculum was developed at TERC (formerly
Technical Education Research Centers) in collaboration with Kent State
University and the State University of New York at Buffalo. The work was
supported in part by National Science Foundation Grant No. ESI-9050210.
TERC is a nonprofit company working to improve mathematics and science
education. TERC is located at 2067 Massachusetts Avenue, Cambridge,
MA 02140.

This project was supported, in part,
by the
National Science Foundation
Opinions expressed are those of the authors
and not necessarily those of the Foundation

Managing Editor: Catherine Anderson

Series Editor: Beverly Cory

Revision Team: Laura Marshall Alavosus, Ellen Harding, Patty Green Holubar,
Suzanne Knott, Beverly Hersh Lozoff

ESL Consultant: Nancy Sokol Green

Production/Manufacturing Director: Janet Yearian

Production/Manufacturing Coordinator: Amy Changar, Shannon Miller

Design Manager: Jeff Kelly

Design: Don Taka

Illustrations: Barbara Epstein-Eagle, Hollis Burkhart

Cover: Bay Graphics

Composition: Archetype Book Composition

This book is published by Dale Seymour Publications®, an imprint of
Addison Wesley Longman, Inc.

Dale Seymour Publications
2725 Sand Hill Road
Menlo Park, CA 94025
Customer Service: 800-872-1100

Order number DS43899
ISBN 1-57232-752-9
4 5 6 7 8 9 10-ML-01 00 99

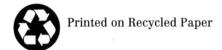

Printed on Recycled Paper

T E R C

INVESTIGATIONS IN NUMBER, DATA, AND SPACE®

Principal Investigator　　Susan Jo Russell

Co-Principal Investigator　　Cornelia C. Tierney

Director of Research and Evaluation　　Jan Mokros

Curriculum Development

Joan Akers
Michael T. Battista
Mary Berle-Carman
Douglas H. Clements
Karen Economopoulos
Ricardo Nemirovsky
Andee Rubin
Susan Jo Russell
Cornelia C. Tierney
Amy Shulman Weinberg

Evaluation and Assessment

Mary Berle-Carman
Abouali Farmanfarmaian
Jan Mokros
Mark Ogonowski
Amy Shulman Weinberg
Tracey Wright
Lisa Yaffee

Teacher Development

Rebecca B. Corwin
Karen Economopoulos
Tracey Wright
Lisa Yaffee

Technology Development

Michael T. Battista
Douglas H. Clements
Julie Sarama Meredith
Andee Rubin

Video Production

David A. Smith

Administration and Production

Amy Catlin
Amy Taber

**Cooperating Classrooms
for This Unit**

Lynn Angelo
Margarette (Peggy) Chudzik
Ruth Kresser
Buffalo Public School System
Buffalo, NY

Barb Dorogi
Cathy Jones
Williamsville Central School District
Williamsville, NY

Kathleen D. O'Connell
Arlington Public Schools
Arlington, MA

Consultants and Advisors

Elizabeth Badger
Deborah Lowenberg Ball
Marilyn Burns
Ann Grady
Joanne M. Gurry
James J. Kaput
Steven Leinwand
Mary M. Lindquist
David S. Moore
John Olive
Leslie P. Steffe
Peter Sullivan
Grayson Wheatley
Virginia Woolley
Anne Zarinnia

Graduate Assistants

Kent State University

Joanne Caniglia
Pam DeLong
Carol King

State University of New York at Buffalo

Rosa Gonzalez
Sue McMillen
Julie Sarama Meredith
Sudha Swaminathan

Revisions and Home Materials

Cathy Miles Grant
Marlene Kliman
Margaret McGaffigan
Megan Murray
Kim O'Neil
Andee Rubin
Susan Jo Russell
Lisa Seyferth
Myriam Steinback
Judy Storeygard
Anna Suarez
Cornelia Tierney
Carol Walker
Tracey Wright

CONTENTS

TEACHER NOTES

WHERE TO START

The first-time user of *Sunken Ships and Grid Patterns* should read the following:

When you next teach this same unit, you can begin to read more of the
background. Each time you present the unit, you will learn more about
how your students understand the mathematical ideas.

Investigations in Number, Data, and Space® is a K–5 mathematics curriculum with four major goals:

- to offer students meaningful mathematical problems
- to emphasize depth in mathematical thinking rather than superficial exposure to a series of fragmented topics
- to communicate mathematics content and pedagogy to teachers
- to substantially expand the pool of mathematically literate students

The *Investigations* curriculum embodies a new approach based on years of research about how children learn mathematics. Each grade level consists of a set of separate units, each offering 2–8 weeks of work. These units of study are presented through investigations that involve students in the exploration of major mathematical ideas.

Approaching the mathematics content through investigations helps students develop flexibility and confidence in approaching problems, fluency in using mathematical skills and tools to solve problems, and proficiency in evaluating their solutions. Students also build a repertoire of ways to communicate about their mathematical thinking, while their enjoyment and appreciation of mathematics grows.

The investigations are carefully designed to invite all students into mathematics—girls and boys, members of diverse cultural, ethnic, and language groups, and students with different strengths and interests. Problem contexts often call on students to share experiences from their family, culture, or community. The curriculum eliminates barriers—such as work in isolation from peers, or emphasis on speed and memorization—that exclude some students from participating successfully in mathematics. The following aspects of the curriculum ensure that all students are included in significant mathematics learning:

- Students spend time exploring problems in depth.
- They find more than one solution to many of the problems they work on.

- They invent their own strategies and approaches, rather than relying on memorized procedures.
- They choose from a variety of concrete materials and appropriate technology, including calculators, as a natural part of their everyday mathematical work.
- They express their mathematical thinking through drawing, writing, and talking.
- They work in a variety of groupings—as a whole class, individually, in pairs, and in small groups.
- They move around the classroom as they explore the mathematics in their environment and talk with their peers.

While reading and other language activities are typically given a great deal of time and emphasis in elementary classrooms, mathematics often does not get the time it needs. If students are to experience mathematics in depth, they must have enough time to become engaged in real mathematical problems. We believe that a minimum of five hours of mathematics classroom time a week—about an hour a day—is critical at the elementary level. The plan and pacing of the *Investigations* curriculum is based on that belief.

We explain more about the pedagogy and principles that underlie these investigations in Teacher Notes throughout the units. For correlations of the curriculum to the NCTM Standards and further help in using this research-based program for teaching mathematics, see the following books:

- *Implementing the* Investigations in Number, Data, and Space® *Curriculum*
- *Beyond Arithmetic: Changing Mathematics in the Elementary Classroom* by Jan Mokros, Susan Jo Russell, and Karen Economopoulos

This book is one of the curriculum units for *Investigations in Number, Data, and Space.* In addition to providing part of a complete mathematics curriculum for your students, this unit offers information to support your own professional development. You, the teacher, are the person who will make this curriculum come alive in the classroom; the book for each unit is your main support system.

Although the curriculum does not include student textbooks, reproducible sheets for student work are provided in the unit and are also available as Student Activity Booklets. Students work actively with objects and experiences in their own environment and with a variety of manipulative materials and technology, rather than with a book of instruction and problems. We strongly recommend use of the overhead projector as a way to present problems, to focus group discussion, and to help students share ideas and strategies.

Ultimately, every teacher will use these investigations in ways that make sense for his or her

particular style, the particular group of students, and the constraints and supports of a particular school environment. Each unit offers information and guidance for a wide variety of situations, drawn from our collaborations with many teachers and students over many years. Our goal in this book is to help you, a professional educator, implement this curriculum in a way that will give all your students access to mathematical power.

Investigation Format

The opening two pages of each investigation help you get ready for the work that follows.

What Happens This gives a synopsis of each session or block of sessions.

Mathematical Emphasis This lists the most important ideas and processes students will encounter in this investigation.

What to Plan Ahead of Time These lists alert you to materials to gather, sheets to duplicate, transparencies to make, and anything else you need to do before starting.

Locating Houses and Ships on a Grid

What Happens

Session 1: Coordinates and Distances on a Grid Students learn how to label points on a coordinate grid with an ordered pair of positive numbers. They choose and describe addresses for their own houses on a grid of streets and avenues. They practice using coordinates by delivering envelopes with partial addresses to people living in Grid City. Students learn the concept of distance on a grid as the length of a "taxi-cab path."

Session 2: Introducing Negative Coordinates Students work with a map of Four-Quadrant City, whose street addresses require negative coordinates. They play Tic-Tac-Toe on the grid to practice with coordinates containing negative numbers. They make up Coordinate Mystery Pictures with negative coordinates and exchange them with other students.

Sessions 3 and 4: Playing Sunken Ships In Session 3, students discuss how to find all locations a given distance away from a point on the grid. They learn to play Sunken Ships both on and off the computer. Then half the class works in pairs playing Sunken Ships on the computer while the other half works in pairs playing the game off the computer. Halfway through the work period the groups switch.

In Session 4, students again play Sunken Ships both on and off the computer. The off-computer group may also make and exchange coordinate mysteries. In the last 30 minutes, the class figures out how to determine the length of the shortest path from the lower-right corner to the upper-left corner of a grid.

Sessions 5 and 6: Distances On and Off the Computer Students learn how to use *Geo-Logo* to draw paths on a grid. They use the On-Computer Activity, Taxi, to find the shortest path

that reaches five different houses and returns home. Off computer, they explore how to find the distance between two points on the grid from the coordinates of the points. In Session 6, all students do the Assessment: Designing a Town during their off-computer time.

Mathematical Emphasis

- Using positive and negative coordinates to name and locate points on grids
- Calculating distances on a grid based on paths along grid lines
- Exploring numerical patterns that represent geometric situations
- Connecting visual and numerical descriptions of distances on a grid

What to Plan Ahead of Time

Materials

- Computers—Macintosh II or above, with 4 MB of internal memory (RAM) and Apple System Software 7.0 or later. Maximum: 1 for every 2 students. Minimum: 1 for every 4–6 students. It is possible to modify the unit for a different number of computers; see Managing the Computer Activities in This Unit (p. I-19).
- Apple Macintosh disk, *Geo-Logo*, for *Sunken Ships and Grid Patterns* (Sessions 3–6)
- Computer disks for students to save their work
- A large-screen monitor on one computer for whole-class viewing (recommended)
- Overhead projector (Sessions 1–6)
- Colored pens for the overhead transparencies (Sessions 1–4)
- Crayons or colored pencils: several per student (Sessions 3–4)

Other Preparation

- Duplicate teaching resources and student sheets, located at the end of the unit, in the following quantities. If you have Student Activity Booklets, copy off the items marked with an asterisk, including any transparencies needed.

For Session 1

Student Sheet 1, Grid City (p. 135): 1 per student, and 1 overhead transparency*

Student Sheet 2, Finding Distances in Grid City (p. 136): 1 per pair

Student Sheet 3, Coordinate Mystery (p. 137): 1 per student

Envelopes* (p. 148): 1 overhead transparency

Family letter* (p. 134): 1 per student. Remember to sign and date it before copying.

For Session 2

Student Sheet 4, Four-Quadrant City Map (p. 138): 1 per student, and 1 overhead transparency*

Student Sheet 5, Grid Paper (p. 139): 3–4 per pair, 1 for homework, and 1 overhead transparency* (optional)

For Sessions 3–4

Student Sheet 6, How to Play Sunken Ships on Paper (p. 140): 2 per student

Geo-Logo User Sheet* (p. 149): 1 per computer

Student Sheet 7, Sunken Ships Grids (p. 141): 3–4 per student, and 1 overhead transparency*

Student Sheet 8, How to Play Sunken Ships on the Computer (p. 142): 1 per pair

Student Sheet 9, Patterns in Paths (p. 143): 1 per student, and 1 overhead transparency*

For Sessions 5–6

Student Sheet 10, Taxi (p. 144): 1 per pair, and 1 overhead transparency*

Student Sheet 11, Distances and Coordinates (p. 145): 1 per pair

Student Sheet 12, Designing a Town (p. 146): 1 per student

Student Sheet 13, Procedure Planning Paper (p. 147): 1 per student

Continued on next page

Sessions Within an investigation, the activities are organized by class session, a session being at least a one-hour math class. Sessions are numbered consecutively through an investigation. Often several sessions are grouped together, presenting a block of activities with a single major focus.

When you find a block of sessions presented together—for example, Sessions 1, 2, and 3—read through the entire block first to understand the overall flow and sequence of the activities. Make some preliminary decisions about how you will divide the activities into three sessions for your class, based on what you know about your students. You may need to modify your initial plans as you progress through the activities, and you may want to make notes in the margins of the pages as reminders for the next time you use the unit.

Be sure to read the Session Follow-Up section at the end of the session block to see what homework assignments and extensions are suggested as you make your initial plans.

While you may be used to a curriculum that tells you exactly what each class session should cover, we have found that the teacher is in a better position to make these decisions. Each unit is flexible and may be handled somewhat differently by every teacher. While we provide guidance for how many sessions a particular group of activities is likely to need, we want you to be active in determining an appropriate pace and the best transition points for your class. It is not unusual for a teacher to spend more or less time than is proposed for the activities.

Ten-Minute Math At the beginning of some sessions, you will find Ten-Minute Math activities. These are designed to be used in tandem with the investigations, but not during the math hour. Rather, we hope you will do them whenever you have a spare 10 minutes—maybe before lunch or recess, or at the end of the day.

Ten-Minute Math offers practice in key concepts, but not always those being covered in the unit. For example, in a unit on using data, Ten-Minute Math might revisit geometric activities done earlier in the year. Complete directions for the suggested activities are included at the end of each unit.

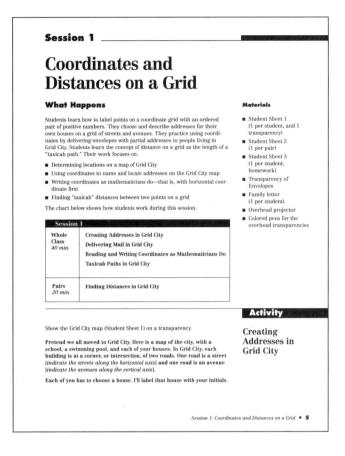

Activities The activities include pair and small-group work, individual tasks, and whole-class discussions. In any case, students are seated together, talking and sharing ideas during all work times. Students most often work cooperatively, although each student may record work individually.

Choice Time In some units, some sessions are structured with activity choices. In these cases, students may work simultaneously on different activities focused on the same mathematical ideas. Students choose which activities they want to do, and they cycle through them.

You will need to decide how to set up and introduce these activities and how to let students make their choices. Some teachers present them as station activities, in different parts of the room. Some list the choices on the board as reminders or have students keep their own lists.

Extensions Sometimes in Session Follow-Up, you will find suggested extension activities. These are opportunities for some or all students to explore a topic in greater depth or in a different context. They are not designed for "fast" students; mathematics is a multifaceted discipline, and different students will want to go further in different investigations. Look for and encourage the sparks of interest and enthusiasm you see in your students, and use the extensions to help them pursue these interests.

Excursions Some of the *Investigations* units include excursions—blocks of activities that could be omitted without harming the integrity of the unit. This is one way of dealing with the great depth and variety of elementary mathematics—much more than a class has time to explore in any one year. Excursions give you the flexibility to make different choices from year to year, doing the excursion in one unit this time, and next year trying another excursion.

Tips for the Linguistically Diverse Classroom At strategic points in each unit, you will find concrete suggestions for simple modifications of the teaching strategies to encourage the participation of all students. Many of these tips offer alternative ways to elicit critical thinking from students at varying levels of English proficiency, as well as from other students who find it difficult to verbalize their thinking.

The tips are supported by suggestions for specific vocabulary work to help ensure that all students can participate fully in the investigations. The Preview for the Linguistically Diverse Classroom (p. I-18) lists important words that are assumed as part of the working vocabulary of the unit. Second-language learners will need to become familiar with these words in order to understand the problems and activities they will be doing. These terms can be incorporated into students' second-language work before or during the unit. Activities that can be used to present the words are found in the appendix, Vocabulary Support for Second-Language Learners (p. 90). In addition, ideas for making connections to students' language and cultures, included on the Preview page, help the class explore the unit's concepts from a multicultural perspective.

Materials

A complete list of the materials needed for teaching this unit is found on p. I-15. Some of these materials are available in kits for the *Investigations* curriculum. Individual items can also be purchased from school supply dealers.

Classroom Materials In an active mathematics classroom, certain basic materials should be available at all times: interlocking cubes, pencils, unlined paper, graph paper, calculators, things to count with, and measuring tools. Some activities in this curriculum require scissors and glue sticks or tape. Stick-on notes and large paper are also useful materials throughout.

So that students can independently get what they need at any time, they should know where these materials are kept, how they are stored, and how they are to be returned to the storage area. For example, interlocking cubes are best stored in towers of ten; then, whatever the activity, they should be returned to storage in groups of ten at the end of the hour. You'll find that establishing such routines at the beginning of the year is well worth the time and effort.

Technology Calculators are used throughout *Investigations.* Many of the units recommend that you have at least one calculator for each pair. You will find calculator activities, plus Teacher Notes discussing this important mathematical tool, in an early unit at each grade level. It is assumed that calculators will be readily available for student use.

Computer activities at grade 4 use a software program that was developed especially for the *Investigations* curriculum. The program *Geo-Logo*™ is used for activities in the 2-D Geometry unit, *Sunken Ships and Grid Patterns,* where students explore coordinate graphing systems, the use of negative numbers to represent locations in space, and the properties of geometric figures.

How you use the computer activities depends on the number of computers you have available. Suggestions are offered in the geometry units for how to organize different types of computer environments.

Children's Literature Each unit offers a list of suggested children's literature (p. I-15) that can be used to support the mathematical ideas in the unit. Sometimes an activity is based on a specific children's book, with suggestions for substitutions where practical. While such activities can be adapted and taught without the book, the literature offers a rich introduction and should be used whenever possible.

Student Sheets and Teaching Resources Student recording sheets and other teaching tools needed for both class and homework are provided as reproducible blackline masters at the end of each unit. They are also available as Student Activity Booklets. These booklets contain all the sheets each student will need for individual work, freeing you from extensive copying (although you may need or want to copy the occasional teaching resource on transparency film or card stock, or make extra copies of a student sheet).

We think it's important that students find their own ways of organizing and recording their work. They need to learn how to explain their thinking with both drawings and written words, and how to organize their results so someone else can under-

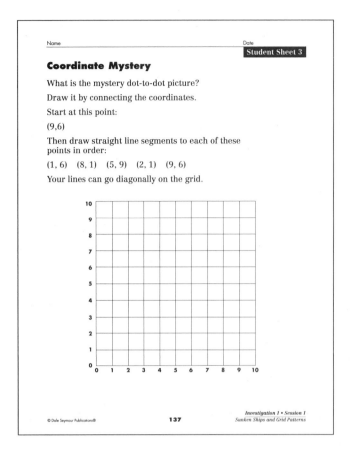

stand them. For this reason, we deliberately do not provide student sheets for every activity. Regardless of the form in which students do their work, we recommend that they keep a mathematics notebook or folder so that their work is always available for reference.

Homework In *Investigations,* homework is an extension of classroom work. Sometimes it offers review and practice of work done in class, sometimes preparation for upcoming activities, and sometimes numerical practice that revisits work in earlier units. Homework plays a role both in supporting students' learning and in helping inform families about the ways in which students in this curriculum work with mathematical ideas.

Depending on your school's homework policies and your own judgment, you may want to assign more homework than is suggested in the units. For this purpose you might use the practice pages, included as blackline masters at the end of this unit, to give students additional work with numbers.

For some homework assignments, you will want to adapt the activity to meet the needs of a variety of students in your class: those with special needs, those ready for more challenge, and second-language learners. You might change the numbers in a problem, make the activity more or less complex, or go through a sample activity with those who need extra help. You can modify any student sheet for either homework or class use. In particular, making numbers in a problem smaller or larger can make the same basic activity appropriate for a wider range of students.

Another issue to consider is how to handle the homework that students bring back to class—how to recognize the work they have done at home without spending too much time on it. Some teachers hold a short group discussion of different approaches to the assignment; others ask students to share and discuss their work with a neighbor, or post the homework around the room and give students time to tour it briefly. If you want to keep track of homework students bring in, be sure it ends up in a designated place.

Investigations at Home It is a good idea to make your policy on homework explicit to both students and their families when you begin teaching with *Investigations*. How frequently will you be assigning homework? When do you expect homework to be completed and brought back to school? What are your goals in assigning homework? How independent should families expect their children to be? What should the parent's or guardian's role be? The more explicit you can be about your expectations, the better the homework experience will be for everyone.

Investigations at Home (a booklet available separately for each unit, to send home with students) gives you a way to communicate with families about the work students are doing in class. This booklet includes a brief description of every session, a list of the mathematics content emphasized in each investigation, and a discussion of each homework assignment to help families more effectively support their children. Whether or not you are using the *Investigations* at Home booklets, we expect you to make your own choices about home-

work assignments. Feel free to omit any and to add extra ones you think are appropriate.

Family Letter A letter that you can send home to students' families is included with the blackline masters for each unit. Families need to be informed about the mathematics work in your classroom; they should be encouraged to participate in and support their children's work. A reminder to send home the letter for each unit appears in one of the early investigations. These letters are also available separately in Spanish, Vietnamese, Cantonese, Hmong, and Cambodian.

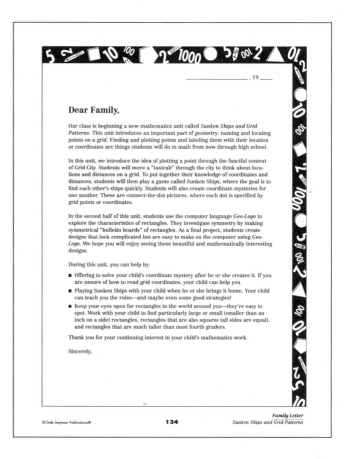

Help for You, the Teacher

Because we believe strongly that a new curriculum must help teachers think in new ways about mathematics and about their students' mathematical thinking processes, we have included a great deal of material to help you learn more about both.

About the Mathematics in This Unit This introductory section (p. I-16) summarizes the critical information about the mathematics you will be teaching. It describes the unit's central mathematical ideas and how students will encounter them through the unit's activities.

Teacher Notes These reference notes provide practical information about the mathematics you are teaching and about our experience with how students learn. Many of the notes were written in response to actual questions from teachers, or to discuss important things we saw happening in the field-test classrooms. Some teachers like to read them all before starting the unit, then review them as they come up in particular investigations.

Dialogue Boxes Sample dialogues demonstrate how students typically express their mathematical ideas, what issues and confusions arise in their thinking, and how some teachers have guided class discussions.

These dialogues are based on the extensive classroom testing of this curriculum; many are word-for-word transcriptions of recorded class discussions. They are not always easy reading; sometimes it may take some effort to unravel what the students are trying to say. But this is the value of these dialogues; they offer good clues to how your students may develop and express their approaches and strategies, helping you prepare for your own class discussions.

Where to Start You may not have time to read everything the first time you use this unit. As a first-time user, you will likely focus on understanding the activities and working them out with your students. Read completely through each investigation before starting to present it. Also read those sections listed in the Contents under the heading Where to Start (p. vi).

Teacher Note *What Are We Measuring?*

In this session, we are measuring distances—the number of blocks, or line segments, along the path.

Here the path between the two houses is 6 blocks long.

Some students, though, may initially think of a "block" as a square region.

Others may count "blocks" by counting each point, or intersection, with the starting point counted as "1."

You may find that having students think in terms of motion, visualizing themselves walking along the roads in the diagram, helps them think about the problem in ways consistent with our definition of "block." You may want some students to act out being a taxi, counting blocks as they drive along streets and avenues.

D I A L O G U E   B O X

Communicating with Negative Numbers

This discussion takes place while students are working on the activity Using Negative Coordinates (p. 11).

What address do you think ZA should have?

Kim: (1, 4).

What address does AB have?

The class: (1, 4).

So where should the mail carrier take a letter addressed (1, 4)?

Kenyana: We should use alphabet letters for that side of the city.

Joey: No! Just reverse the coordinates! Say (4, 1) instead of (1, 4).

Sarah: That wouldn't work! What about the (4, 1) over on the east!

Rafael: I think, if you were counting, 8, 7, 6, 5, 4, 3, 2, 1, 0, then minus 1, minus 2. . . .

So, use negative numbers?

Rafael: Yes. Just go the other way.

Later, the teacher notices that some students sometimes drop the word *negative*. She decides that the best teaching strategy would be to emphasize communication failures this might cause. This happens when Jesse is naming a point to which *UV* could have walked.

Jesse: *UV* could have walked to (2, 3).

[The teacher purposely begins gesturing to mark the point (2, 3).]

Jesse: No! Not there!

Oh, what did you say? (2, 3)?

Jesse: Yeah. Oh! (2, –3).

Ah-ha! (2, –3). Now I understand you.

The *Investigations* curriculum incorporates the use of two forms of technology in the classroom: calculators and computers. Calculators are assumed to be standard classroom materials, available for student use in any unit. Computers are explicitly linked to one or more units at each grade level; they are used with the unit on 2-D geometry at each grade, as well as with some of the units on measuring, data, and changes.

Using Calculators

In this curriculum, calculators are considered tools for doing mathematics, similar to pattern blocks or interlocking cubes. Just as with other tools, students must learn both *how* to use calculators correctly and *when* they are appropriate to use. This knowledge is crucial for daily life, as calculators are now a standard way of handling numerical operations, both at work and at home.

Using a calculator correctly is not a simple task; it depends on a good knowledge of the four operations and of the number system, so that students can select suitable calculations and also determine what a reasonable result would be. These skills are the basis of any work with numbers, whether or not a calculator is involved.

Unfortunately, calculators are often seen as tools to check computations with, as if other methods are somehow more fallible. Students need to understand that any computational method can be used to check any other; it's just as easy to make a mistake on the calculator as it is to make a mistake on paper or with mental arithmetic. Throughout this curriculum, we encourage students to solve computation problems in more than one way in order to double-check their accuracy. We present mental arithmetic, paper-and-pencil computation, and calculators as three possible approaches.

In this curriculum we also recognize that, despite their importance, calculators are not always appropriate in mathematics instruction. Like any tools, calculators are useful for some tasks, but not for others. You will need to make decisions about when to allow students access to calculators and when to ask that they solve problems without them, so that they can concentrate on other tools and skills. At times when calculators are or are not appropriate for a particular activity, we make specific recommendations. Help your students develop their own sense of which problems they can tackle with their own reasoning and which ones might be better solved with a combination of their own reasoning and the calculator.

Managing calculators in your classroom so that they are a tool, and not a distraction, requires some planning. When calculators are first introduced, students often want to use them for everything, even problems that can be solved quite simply by other methods. However, once the novelty wears off, students are just as interested in developing their own strategies, especially when these strategies are emphasized and valued in the classroom. Over time, students will come to recognize the ease and value of solving problems mentally, with paper and pencil, or with manipulatives, while also understanding the power of the calculator to facilitate work with larger numbers.

Experience shows that if calculators are available only occasionally, students become excited and distracted when they are permitted to use them. They focus on the tool rather than on the mathematics. In order to learn when calculators are appropriate and when they are not, students must have easy access to them and use them routinely in their work.

If you have a calculator for each student, and if you think your students can accept the responsibility, you might allow them to keep their calculators with the rest of their individual materials, at least for the first few weeks of school. Alternatively, you might store them in boxes on a shelf, number each calculator, and assign a corresponding number to each student. This system can give students a sense of ownership while also helping you keep track of the calculators.

Using Computers

Students can use computers to approach and visualize mathematical situations in new ways. The computer allows students to construct and manipulate geometric shapes, see objects move according to rules they specify, and turn, flip, and repeat a pattern.

This curriculum calls for computers in units where they are a particularly effective tool for learning mathematics content. One unit on 2-D geometry at each of the grades 3–5 includes a core of activities that rely on access to computers, either in the classroom or in a lab. Other units on geometry, measurement, data, and changes include computer activities, but can be taught without them. In these units, however, students' experience is greatly enhanced by computer use.

The following list outlines the recommended use of computers in this curriculum:

Grade 1
Unit: *Survey Questions and Secret Rules*
   (Collecting and Sorting Data)
Software: Tabletop, Jr.
Source: Broderbund

Unit: *Quilt Squares and Block Towns*
   (2-D and 3-D Geometry)
Software: *Shapes*
Source: provided with the unit

Grade 2
Unit: *Mathematical Thinking at Grade 2*
   (Introduction)
Software: *Shapes*
Source: provided with the unit

Unit: *Shapes, Halves, and Symmetry*
   (Geometry and Fractions)
Software: *Shapes*
Source: provided with the unit

Unit: *How Long? How Far?* (Measuring)
Software: *Geo-Logo*
Source: provided with the unit

Grade 3
Unit: *Flips, Turns, and Area* (2-D Geometry)
Software: *Tumbling Tetrominoes*
Source: provided with the unit

Unit: *Turtle Paths* (2-D Geometry)
Software: *Geo-Logo*
Source: provided with the unit

Grade 4
Unit: *Sunken Ships and Grid Patterns*
   (2-D Geometry)
Software: *Geo-Logo*
Source: provided with the unit

Grade 5
Unit: *Picturing Polygons* (2-D Geometry)
Software: *Geo-Logo*
Source: provided with the unit

Unit: *Patterns of Change* (Tables and Graphs)
Software: *Trips*
Source: provided with the unit

Unit: *Data: Kids, Cats, and Ads* (Statistics)
Software: Tabletop, Sr.
Source: Broderbund

The software provided with the *Investigations* units uses the power of the computer to help students explore mathematical ideas and relationships that cannot be explored in the same way with physical materials. With the *Shapes* (grades 1–2) and *Tumbling Tetrominoes* (grade 3) software, students explore symmetry, pattern, rotation and reflection, area, and characteristics of 2-D shapes. With the *Geo-Logo* software (grades 3–5), students investigate rotations and reflections, coordinate geometry, the properties of 2-D shapes, and angles. The *Trips* software (grade 5) is a mathematical exploration of motion in which students run experiments and interpret data presented in graphs and tables.

We suggest that students work in pairs on the computer; this not only maximizes computer resources but also encourages students to consult, monitor, and teach one another. Generally, more than two students at one computer find it difficult to share. Managing access to computers is an issue for every classroom. The curriculum gives you explicit support for setting up a system. The units are structured on the assumption that you have enough computers for half your students to work on the machines in pairs at one time. If you do not have access to that many computers, suggestions are made for structuring class time to use the unit with five to eight computers, or even with fewer than five.

Assessment plays a critical role in teaching and learning, and it is an integral part of the *Investigations* curriculum. For a teacher using these units, assessment is an ongoing process. You observe students' discussions and explanations of their strategies on a daily basis and examine their work as it evolves. While students are busy recording and representing their work, working on projects, sharing with partners, and playing mathematical games, you have many opportunities to observe their mathematical thinking. What you learn through observation guides your decisions about how to proceed. In any of the units, you will repeatedly consider questions like these:

- Do students come up with their own strategies for solving problems, or do they expect others to tell them what to do? What do their strategies reveal about their mathematical understanding?

- Do students understand that there are different strategies for solving problems? Do they articulate their strategies and try to understand other students' strategies?

- How effectively do students use materials as tools to help with their mathematical work?

- Do students have effective ideas for keeping track of and recording their work? Does keeping track of and recording their work seem difficult for them?

You will need to develop a comfortable and efficient system for recording and keeping track of your observations. Some teachers keep a clipboard handy and jot notes on a class list or on adhesive labels that are later transferred to student files. Others keep loose-leaf notebooks with a page for each student and make weekly notes about what they have observed in class.

Assessment Tools in the Unit

With the activities in each unit, you will find questions to guide your thinking while observing the students at work. You will also find two built-in assessment tools: Teacher Checkpoints and embedded Assessment activities.

Teacher Checkpoints The designated Teacher Checkpoints in each unit offer a time to "check in" with individual students, watch them at work, and ask questions that illuminate how they are thinking.

At first it may be hard to know what to look for, hard to know what kinds of questions to ask. Students may be reluctant to talk; they may not be accustomed to having the teacher ask them about their work, or they may not know how to explain their thinking. Two important ingredients of this process are asking students open-ended questions about their work and showing genuine interest in how they are approaching the task. When students see that you are interested in their thinking and are counting on them to come up with their own ways of solving problems, they may surprise you with the depth of their understanding.

Teacher Checkpoints also give you the chance to pause in the teaching sequence and reflect on how your class is doing overall. Think about whether you need to adjust your pacing: Are most students fluent with strategies for solving a particular kind of problem? Are they just starting to formulate good strategies? Or are they still struggling with how to start? Depending on what you see as the students work, you may want to spend more time on similar problems, change some of the problems to use smaller numbers, move quickly to more challenging material, modify subsequent activities for some students, work on particular ideas with a small group, or pair students who have good strategies with those who are having more difficulty.

Embedded Assessment Activities Assessment activities embedded in each unit will help you examine specific pieces of student work, figure out what it means, and provide feedback. From the students' point of view, these assessment activities are no different from any others. Each is a learning experience in and of itself, as well as an opportunity for you to gather evidence about students' mathematical understanding.

The embedded assessment activities sometimes involve writing and reflecting; at other times, a discussion or brief interaction between student and teacher; and in still other instances, the creation and explanation of a product. In most cases, the assessments require that students *show* what they did, *write* or *talk* about it, or do both. Having to explain how they worked through a problem helps students be more focused and clear in their mathematical thinking. It also helps them realize that doing mathematics is a process that may involve tentative starts, revising one's approach, taking different paths, and working through ideas.

Teachers often find the hardest part of assessment to be interpreting their students' work. We provide guidelines to help with that interpretation. If you have used a process approach to teaching writing, the assessment in *Investigations* will seem familiar. For many of the assessment activities, a Teacher Note provides examples of student work and a commentary on what it indicates about student thinking.

Documentation of Student Growth

To form an overall picture of mathematical progress, it is important to document each student's work in journals, notebooks, or portfolios. The choice is largely a matter of personal preference; some teachers have students keep a notebook or folder for each unit, while others prefer one mathematics notebook, or a portfolio of selected work for the entire year. The final activity in each *Investigations* unit, called Choosing Student Work to Save, helps you and the students select representative samples for a record of their work.

This kind of regular documentation helps you synthesize information about each student as a mathematical learner. From different pieces of evidence, you can put together the big picture. This synthesis will be invaluable in thinking about where to go next with a particular child, deciding where more work is needed, or explaining to parents (or other teachers) how a child is doing.

If you use portfolios, you need to collect a good balance of work, yet avoid being swamped with an overwhelming amount of paper. Following are some tips for effective portfolios:

- Collect a representative sample of work, including some pieces that students themselves select for inclusion in the portfolio. There should be just a few pieces for each unit, showing different kinds of work—some assignments that involve writing, as well as some that do not.

- If students do not date their work, do so yourself so that you can reconstruct the order in which pieces were done.

- Include your reflections on the work. When you are looking back over the whole year, such comments are reminders of what seemed especially interesting about a particular piece; they can also be helpful to other teachers and to parents. Older students should be encouraged to write their own reflections about their work.

Assessment Overview

There are two places to turn for a preview of the assessment opportunities in each *Investigations* unit. The Assessment Resources column in the unit Overview Chart (pp. I-13–I-14) identifies the Teacher Checkpoints and Assessment activities embedded in each investigation, guidelines for observing the students that appear within classroom activities, and any Teacher Notes and Dialogue Boxes that explain what to look for and what types of student responses you might expect to see in your classroom. Additionally, the section About the Assessment in This Unit (p. I-17) gives you a detailed list of questions for each investigation, keyed to the mathematical emphases, to help you observe student growth.

Depending on your situation, you may want to provide additional assessment opportunities. Most of the investigations lend themselves to more frequent assessment, simply by having students do more writing and recording while they are working.

Sunken Ships and Grid Patterns

Content of This Unit   Students name and locate points on a coordinate grid with ordered pairs of numbers, both positive and negative. They make coordinate mystery pictures and measure distances on the grid using "taxicab paths." They play Sunken Ships, identifying points on the grid and using distance feedback in their strategy for selecting a next possible location. Students discuss properties of rectangles and write rectangle procedures for the computer using *Geo-Logo*. They place rectangles symmetrically on a computer bulletin board. They analyze a general *Geo-Logo* procedure for making rectangles and use the procedure to draw and create complex rectangle patterns.

Note: This unit makes substantial use of computers. It is important to read Managing the Computer Activities in This Unit (p. I-19) and go through the *Geo-Logo* Teacher Tutorial (p. 91), prior to teaching this unit.

Connection with Other Units   If you are doing the full-year *Investigations* curriculum in the suggested sequence for grade 4, this is the tenth of eleven units. In the unit *Landmarks in the Thousands*, your students worked with negative numbers in the scoring system for the game Close to 1000. They met grids in the *Changes Over Time* unit. If your students have not had comparable experiences, you may need to spend more time on the first few sessions where students learn about the structure of a grid and how negative numbers are used to locate points. If your students have used the third-grade units, they have worked with *Geo-Logo* on the computer in the 2-D Geometry unit *Turtle Paths*. Students may also have had experience with *Geo-Logo* in the second grade units *Introduction to Mathematical Thinking at Grade 2* and *How Long? How Far?* If so, they may be able to complete *Geo-Logo* tasks in less time.

If your school is not using the full-year curriculum, this unit can also be used successfully at grade 5, depending on the previous experience and needs of your students.

Investigations Curriculum   ■   Suggested Grade 4 Sequence

Mathematical Thinking at Grade 4 (Introduction)

Arrays and Shares (Multiplication and Division)

Seeing Solids and Silhouettes (3-D Geometry)

Landmarks in the Thousands (The Number System)

Different Shapes, Equal Pieces (Fractions and Area)

The Shape of the Data (Statistics)

Money, Miles, and Large Numbers (Addition and Subtraction)

Changes Over Time (Graphs)

Packages and Groups (Multiplication and Division)

▶ *Sunken Ships and Grid Patterns* (2-D Geometry)

Three out of Four Like Spaghetti (Data and Fractions)

Investigation 1 ■ Locating Houses and Ships on a Grid

Class Sessions	Activities	Pacing
Session 1 (p. 5) COORDINATES AND DISTANCES ON A GRID	Creating Addresses in Grid City Delivering Mail in Grid City Reading and Writing Coordinates as Mathematicians Do Taxicab Paths in Grid City Finding Distances in Grid City Homework: Coordinate Mystery	minimum 1 hr
Session 2 (p. 11) INTRODUCING NEGATIVE COORDINATES	Using Negative Coordinates Playing Grid Tic-Tac-Toe Coordinate Mystery Pictures Homework: Coordinate Mystery or Grid Tic-Tac-Toe	minimum 1 hr

Sessions 3 and 4 (p. 17)
PLAYING SUNKEN SHIPS
	Introducing Work Procedures
	Finding All Locations a Given Distance Away
	Off-Computer Activity: Playing Sunken Ships on Paper
	On-Computer Activity: Playing Sunken Ships on
	    the Computer
	Teacher Checkpoint: Students' Use of Coordinates
	    and Distances
	Discussing Sunken Ships Strategies
	Shortest Paths on a Grid
	Homework: Sunken Ships
	Homework: Patterns in Paths
	Extension: More Sunken Ships
		minimum
		2 hr

Sessions 5 and 6 (p. 30) DISTANCES ON AND OFF THE COMPUTER	Discussing Shortest Paths Introducing *Geo-Logo* Movement Commands On-Computer Activity: Taxi Off-Computer Activity: Distances and Coordinates Using Coordinates to Find Distances Assessment: Designing a Town Extension: Distances with Negative Coordinates	minimum 2 hr

🕐 **Ten-Minute Math ■ Lengths and Perimeters**

Mathematical Emphasis

- Using positive and negative coordinates to name and locate points on a grid

- Calculating distances on a grid based on paths along grid lines

- Exploring numerical patterns that represent geometric situations

- Connecting visual and numerical descriptions of distances on a grid

Assessment Resources

What Are We Measuring? (Teacher Note, p. 10)

Communicating with Negative Numbers (Dialogue Box, p. 16)

Teacher Checkpoint: Students' Use of Coordinates and Distances (p. 23)

Guessing Smart with Mathematical Thinking (Dialogue Box, p. 28)

Assessment: Designing a Town (p. 37)

Patterns, Predictions, and Reasons (Dialogue Box, p. 41)

Materials

Computers

Computer disks

Large-screen monitor

Overhead projector

Colored pens

Crayons or colored pencils

Family letter

Student Sheets 1–13

Teaching resource sheets

Investigation 2 ▪ Rectangles, Turns, and Coordinates

Class Sessions	Activities	Pacing
Session 1 (p. 45) MAKING RECTANGLES	Identifying and Drawing Rectangles On-Computer Activity: Writing Rectangle Procedures Off-Computer Choices: Finding Rectangles Homework: What Is a Rectangle?	minimum 1 hr

Sessions 2 and 3 (p. 51)
RECTANGLES, COORDINATES,
AND SYMMETRY
	Placing Rectangles on a Grid
	On-Computer Activity: Symmetrical Bulletin Boards
	Off-Computer Choices: Planning Symmetrical
	    Bulletin Boards
	Teacher Checkpoint: Making Symmetrical
	    Bulletin Boards
	Discussing Symmetrical Patterns
	Homework: Symmetry in the World
	Homework: Drawing More Symmetrical Patterns
		minimum
		2 hr

Session 4 (p. 58) PROPERTIES OF RECTANGLES	Analyzing Rectangles Introducing the rect Procedure On-Computer/Off-Computer Activity: Planning and Drawing Grid Pictures Using the rect Procedure Extension: Using Computer Tools to Analyze Rectangles Extension: That's a "Piece of Cake"	minimum 1 hr
Session 5 (p. 67) TURNS	Off-Computer Activity: Analyzing Rectangle Procedures Turning Your Body	minimum 1 hr
Sessions 6 and 7 (p. 73) TURNING AND REPEATING RECTANGLES	Turning Rectangles Repeating Rectangles On-Computer Activity: Exploring Turns and the repeat Command Off-Computer Activity: Assessment: Am I a Rectangle? Extension: Computer Rectangles Challenge	minimum 2 hr

Sessions 8 and 9 (p. 79)
DESIGNING RECTANGLE PATTERNS
	On-Computer Activity: *Geo-Logo* Rectangle Patterns
	Off-Computer Activity: Drawing Rectangle Patterns
	Teacher Checkpoint: Designing *Geo-Logo*
	    Rectangle Patterns
	Discussing *Geo-Logo* Rectangle Patterns
	Choosing Student Work to Save
	Homework: Grids on Real Maps
	Extensions: *Geo-Logo* Project; Longitude and Latitude;
	    Checkers by Mail
		minimum
		2 hr

🕐 **Ten-Minute Math** ▪ **Lengths and Perimeters**

Mathematical Emphasis

- Applying knowledge of coordinates to locate points on a computer screen
- Describing geometric figures such as rectangles and squares
- Understanding how *Geo-Logo* commands reflect the properties of geometric figures
- Creating and applying patterns and mental arithmetic strategies to solve turtle geometry problems
- Using symmetry to place rectangles on a grid and design complex patterns of rectangles

Assessment Resources

Teacher Checkpoint: Making Symmetrical Bulletin Boards (p. 56)

Pattern and Symmetry (Teacher Note, p. 57)

Turns and Angles (Teacher Note, p. 72)

Assessment: Am I a Rectangle? (p. 76)

What's a Rectangle? What's Not? (Teacher Note, p. 77)

Writing About Rectangles (Teacher Note, p. 78)

Teacher Checkpoint: Designing *Geo-Logo* Rectangle Patterns (p. 82)

Choosing Student Work to Save (p. 83)

Materials

Computers

Computer disks

Geo-Logo software

Printer

Rulers

Scissors

Overhead projector

Student Sheets 13–28

Teaching resource sheets

Following are the basic materials needed for the activities in this unit. Many of the items can be purchased from the publisher, either individually or in the Teacher Resource Package and the Student Materials Kit for grade 4. Detailed information is available on the *Investigations* order form. To obtain this form, call toll-free 1-800-872-1100 and ask for a Dale Seymour customer representative.

Computers—Macintosh II or above, with 4 MB of internal memory (RAM) and Apple System Software 7.0 or later. Maximum: 1 for every 2 students. Minimum: 1 for every 5–8 students. It is possible to modify the unit for fewer computers (see Managing the Computer Activities in This Unit, p. I-19).

Apple Macintosh disk, *Geo-Logo*, for *Sunken Ships and Grid Patterns* (packaged with this book)

A large-screen monitor on one computer for whole-class viewing (recommended)

Printer (optional)

Overhead projector

Colored pens for the overhead transparencies

Colored pencils or crayons

Rulers, yardsticks, metersticks, or string

Calculators (for Ten-Minute Math, optional)

Scissors

The following materials are provided at the end of this unit as blackline masters. A Student Activity Booklet containing all student sheets and teacher resources needed for individual work is available.

Family Letter (p. 134)

Student Sheets 1–28 (p. 135)

Teaching Resources

    Envelopes (p. 148)

    Geo-Logo User Sheet (p. 149)

    Which Are Rectangles? (p. 168)

    360 Degrees (p. 169)

    Turtle Turners (p. 170)

Practice Pages (p. 171)

Related Children's Literature

Raphael, Elaine, and Dan Bolognese. *Sam Baker, Gone West.* New York: Viking, 1977.

Mathematics is about structure, but too many people think only about the structure of numbers. It is also about the structures of space and shapes. In this unit, students structure two-dimensional space with grids and coordinates. They look for patterns in these spatial structures and explore shapes, particularly rectangles, that are embedded in the grid structure. The activities in this unit develop students' geometric knowledge and their spatial visualization.

An understanding of coordinate systems is important not only for work with maps and two-dimensional space but also for reading and constructing graphs and, later, for graphing functions. So this unit connects strongly with other mathematical topics as well as with other subjects, such as social studies, science, and language arts.

There are several mathematical ideas emphasized in the unit. The first idea is that grids can be used to determine locations in a plane. Further, coordinates can be used for naming and locating points on this grid.

The second is the idea of negative numbers representing locations in space. Negative numbers can be used to extend coordinate grids in all directions. This same way of specifying points can be used on the computer.

The third is the idea that geometric figures, such as rectangles, can be described in several ways. One way is to describe the properties of rectangles, such as having two pairs of sides that are the same length and four 90° angles. The second is through the process of drawing the figure. The *Geo-Logo* commands that form a rectangle reflect these same properties.

From making paths on a grid to working with *Geo-Logo* rectangles, students encounter powerful connections between geometry and number—the fourth idea. Number patterns can be used to describe geometric situations. Geometric patterns can be used to find, illustrate, and better understand number patterns.

The fifth idea is that patterns are what mathematics is all about. Mathematics has been defined as patterns in number, data, and space. The idea of patterns and the use of mathematical clues and strategies to understand patterns form the foundation of this unit.

Mathematical Emphasis At the beginning of each investigation, the Mathematical Emphasis section tells you what is most important for students to learn about during that investigation. Many of these mathematical understandings and processes are difficult and complex. Students gradually learn more and more about each idea over many years of schooling. Individual students will begin and end the unit with different levels of knowledge and skill, but all will gain greater knowledge of two-dimensional space and shape and develop strategies for solving problems involving these ideas.

Throughout the *Investigations* curriculum, there are many opportunities for ongoing daily assessment as you observe, listen to, and interact with students at work. In this unit, you will find three Teacher Checkpoints:

Investigation 1, Sessions 3–4:
Students' Use of Coordinates and Distances (p. 23)

Investigation 2, Sessions 2–3:
Making Symmetrical Bulletin Boards (p. 56)

Investigation 2, Session 8–9
Designing *Geo-Logo* Rectangle Patterns (p. 82)

This unit also has two embedded assessment activities:

Investigation 1, Sessions 5–6:
Designing a Town (p. 37)

Investigation 2, Sessions 6–7:
Am I a Rectangle? (p. 76)

In addition, you can use almost any activity in this unit to assess your students' needs and strengths. Listed below are questions to help you focus your observation in each investigation. You may want to keep track of your observations for each student to help you plan your curriculum and monitor students' growth. Suggestions for documenting student growth can be found in the section About Assessment (p. I-10).

Investigation 1: Locating Houses and Ships on a Grid

■ Are students able to designate a position on a grid by naming its positive and negative coordinates? Given a set of coordinates, can they identify the corresponding point on a grid?

■ How do students think about measuring the distance of a path on a grid? When they measure the number of "blocks," do they count the square regions along one side of the path, resulting in too small a total if the path turns? Do they get too large a total by counting each point or intersection along the path, including the starting point? Are they able to count accurately the number of line segments along the path?

■ What methods do students use to determine the shortest distance between two points on a grid? What numerical patterns do they notice in calcu-lating the number of blocks in the shortest path for different square grids?

■ Can students figure out distances with both positive and negative coordinates? Can they figure out which points are more and less than a certain distance apart?

Investigation 2: Rectangles, Turns, and Coordinates

■ How do students apply their knowledge of coordinates to locate points on the computer screen? Do they guess randomly when trying to position a shape in a certain place, or do they figure out coordinates?

■ In what different ways do students define geometric shapes such as rectangles and squares?

■ How do students approach the symmetry problem of placing a rectangle in the same place in all four quadrants of a grid? Are students able to see and explain why something is or is not symmetrical?

■ What similarities and differences do students observe among *Geo-Logo* procedures for different kinds of rectangles? Can students analyze *Geo-Logo* procedures to determine which will produce rectangles and which won't?

■ What strategies do students use to write *Geo-Logo* procedures? Do they use numerical patterns in their procedures as shortcuts for creating spatial patterns on the screen?

■ How do students demonstrate an understanding of mirror and rotational symmetry in their designs they make with rectangles? Are they able to analyze where to place shapes by using the relationships among coordinates in the four quadrants? Do they need to fold their planning paper in order to do this?

In the *Investigations* curriculum, mathematical vocabulary is introduced naturally during the activities. We don't ask students to learn definitions of new terms; rather, they come to understand such words as *factor*, *area*, and *symmetry* by hearing them used frequently in discussion as they investigate new concepts. This approach is compatible with current theories of second-language acquisition, which emphasize the use of new vocabulary in meaningful contexts while students are actively involved with objects, pictures, and physical movement.

Listed below are some key words used in this unit that will not be new to most English speakers at this age level but may be unfamiliar to students with limited English proficiency. You will want to spend additional time working on these words with your students who are learning English. If your students are working with a second-language teacher, you might enlist your colleague's aid in familiarizing students with these words before and during this unit. In the classroom, look for opportunities for students to hear and use these words. Activities you can use to present the words are given in the appendix, Vocabulary Support for Second-Language Learners (p. 90).

mail carrier, post office, address, letters, deliver Students use the idea of delivering letters to talk about locations in Grid City. Locations in Grid City are specified by two numbers—a street number and an avenue number.

ship, sink, sunk Students play a game called Sunken Ships in which they try to find ships that have sunk under the ocean.

Multicultural Extensions for All Students

Whenever possible, encourage students to share words, objects, customs, or any aspects of daily life from their own cultures and backgrounds that are relevant to the activities in this unit. For example:

- Students can make up Coordinate Mysteries that turn out to be pictures of cultural symbols or cultural objects found in their homes or neighborhoods, such as decorations or flags.

- When students bring in symmetrical objects from home, suggest they try to find objects other students may not be familiar with.

This unit is dependent on having students use computers on an ongoing basis. Ideally, students, working in pairs, will use computers daily for approximately 20 (or more) minutes. This means that you will need to plan carefully so all students have ample time to do the computer activities.

We have structured this unit as if you have five to eight computers in your classroom, enough so that half of your students, working in pairs, can use them at one time. At present, few classrooms have access to this many computers, but we have chosen to write the unit in this way for two reasons: (1) Having five to eight computers available all day in your classroom is most conducive to effective and efficient use of these resources, and (2) writing the unit in this way provides a model for the way computers may be integrated in classrooms in the near future.

We have also provided advice below on how to modify the management of computer resources in two other common situations: where there are fewer than five computers available during math period and where there is a computer laboratory available outside the classroom.

Structuring the Unit to Match Computer Availability

Five to Eight Computers With five to eight computers, half the class, working in pairs, can use them at once. In each session, following a whole-class discussion, half the students do an On-Computer Activity and the other half do an Off-Computer Choice. The two groups switch halfway through the work time. (Continuing to allow pairs of students to work at the computers throughout the school day will provide opportunities for students to complete all the computer activities plus extra time to redo some activities using different commands or strategies.)

Computer Laboratory If you have a computer laboratory, you may wish to involve the whole class in computer activities at the same time. Specific suggestions for modifying the sessions for a computer laboratory are found in the What to Plan Ahead of Time for each investigation. (See pp. 4 and 44.)

Fewer than Five Computers If you have fewer than five computers available to use during the math period, it is mandatory that students rotate using the computers throughout the school day, so every pair has completed the activities before the follow-up discussion. With this strategy, you will always introduce computer activities before the Off-Computer Activities. Students can begin cycling through the computer activity as you work with the remainder of the class on the Off-Computer Activities. Specific suggestions for how to do this are included in the overview for each investigation.

Working at the Computer

Working in Pairs Students should work in pairs on the computers. Working in pairs not only maximizes computer resources but also encourages students to consult, monitor, and teach each other. Generally, more than two students at one computer find it difficult to share. (If you have an odd number of students, a threesome can be formed.) Since frequently students will not complete their computer work in one session, we suggest they stay with the same partner for the entire unit.

Saving Student Work Students will need to save their work in many of the computer activities. This can be done in two ways: (1) Students can use the same computer each time and save their work on the computer's internal drive, or (2) students can save their work on their own disk that they can use on any computer. If you can provide pairs of students with their own disks, computer management will be simpler, because each pair will be able to use any computer when it is available. If students' work is saved on a particular computer, they may have to wait until other students using that computer are finished with their work. Instructions for saving work are on p. 106 of the *Geo-Logo* Teacher Tutorial.

Demonstrating Computer Activities Frequently you will need to use a computer with the whole class to demonstrate computer activities and to share results during whole-class discussions. It is helpful if a computer is connected to a large-screen monitor or projection device—a "large display." If you do not have a large display available, we suggest you gather groups of students as close as possible around the computer. Increasing the font size when entering commands will make them more visible for any demonstrations. To increase the font size, choose **All Large** under the **Font** menu. (When you are finished demonstrating, remember to return the font to its regular size by choosing **All Small** under the **Font** menu.)

If your computer display is very small and it is difficult for your students to see the computer demonstrations, you may want to make a transparency of some of the student sheets that include the computer screen to show students the commands you are entering.

Investigations

Locating Houses and Ships on a Grid

What Happens

Session 1: Coordinates and Distances on a Grid Students learn how to label points on a coordinate grid with an ordered pair of positive numbers. They choose and describe addresses for their own houses on a grid of streets and avenues. They practice using coordinates by delivering envelopes with partial addresses to people living in Grid City. Students learn the concept of distance on a grid as the length of a "taxi-cab path."

Session 2: Introducing Negative Coordinates Students work with a map of Four-Quadrant City, whose street addresses require negative coordinates. They play Tic-Tac-Toe on the grid to practice with coordinates containing negative numbers. They make up Coordinate Mystery Pictures with negative coordinates and exchange them with other students.

Sessions 3 and 4: Playing Sunken Ships In Session 3, students discuss how to find all locations a given distance away from a point on the grid. They learn to play Sunken Ships both on and off the computer. Then half the class works in pairs playing Sunken Ships on the computer while the other half works in pairs playing the game off the computer. Halfway through the work period the groups switch.

In Session 4, students again play Sunken Ships both on and off the computer. The off-computer group may also make and exchange coordinate mysteries. In the last 30 minutes, the class figures out how to determine the length of the shortest path from the lower-right corner to the upper-left corner of a grid.

Sessions 5 and 6: Distances On and Off the Computer Students learn how to use *Geo-Logo* to draw paths on a grid. They use the On-Computer Activity, Taxi, to find the shortest path

that reaches five different houses and returns home. Off computer, they explore how to find the distance between two points on the grid from the coordinates of the points. In Session 6, all students do the Assessment: Designing a Town during their off-computer time.

Mathematical Emphasis

- Using positive and negative coordinates to name and locate points on grids
- Calculating distances on a grid based on paths along grid lines
- Exploring numerical patterns that represent geometric situations
- Connecting visual and numerical descriptions of distances on a grid

What to Plan Ahead of Time

Materials

- Computers—Macintosh II or above, with 4 MB of internal memory (RAM) and Apple System Software 7.0 or later. Maximum: 1 for every 2 students. Minimum: 1 for every 4–6 students. It is possible to modify the unit for a different number of computers; see Managing the Computer Activities in This Unit (p. I-19).

- Apple Macintosh disk, *Geo-Logo*, for *Sunken Ships and Grid Patterns* (Sessions 3–6)

- Computer disks for students to save their work

- A large-screen monitor on one computer for whole-class viewing (recommended)

- Overhead projector (Sessions 1–6)

- Colored pens for the overhead transparencies (Sessions 1–4)

- Crayons or colored pencils: several per student (Sessions 3–4)

Other Preparation

- Duplicate teaching resources and student sheets, located at the end of the unit, in the following quantities. If you have Student Activity Booklets, copy only the items marked with an asterisk, including any transparencies needed.

For Session 1

Student Sheet 1, Grid City (p. 135): 1 per student, and 1 overhead transparency*

Student Sheet 2, Finding Distances in Grid City (p. 136): 1 per pair

Student Sheet 3, Coordinate Mystery (p. 137): 1 per student

Envelopes* (p. 148): 1 overhead transparency

Family letter* (p. 134): 1 per student. Remember to sign and date it before copying.

For Session 2

Student Sheet 4, Four-Quadrant City Map (p. 138): 1 per student, and 1 overhead transparency*

Student Sheet 5, Grid Paper (p. 139): 3–4 per pair, 1 for homework, and 1 overhead transparency* (optional)

For Sessions 3–4

Student Sheet 6, How to Play Sunken Ships on Paper (p. 140): 2 per student

Geo-Logo User Sheet* (p. 149): 1 per computer

Student Sheet 7, Sunken Ships Grids (p. 141): 3–4 per student, and 1 overhead transparency*

Student Sheet 8, How to Play Sunken Ships on the Computer (p. 142): 1 per pair

Student Sheet 9, Patterns in Paths (p. 143): 1 per student, and 1 overhead transparency*

For Sessions 5–6

Student Sheet 10, Taxi (p. 144): 1 per pair, and 1 overhead transparency*

Student Sheet 11, Distances and Coordinates (p. 145): 1 per pair

Student Sheet 12, Designing a Town (p. 146): 1 per student

Student Sheet 13, Procedure Planning Paper (p. 147): 1 per student

Continued on next page

What to Plan Ahead of Time (*continued*)

■ Use the disk for *Sunken Ships and Grid Patterns* to install *Geo-Logo* on each computer. (See p. 130 in the *Geo-Logo* Teacher Tutorial.)

■ Work through the following sections of the *Geo-Logo* Teacher Tutorial

■ Plan how to manage the computer activities.

If you have five to eight computers, follow the investigation structure as written.

If you have a computer laboratory, spend two sessions on the noncomputer activities, then one session in the computer lab, completing both On-Computer Activities, Sunken Ships and Taxi. If you need to keep your computer days consecutive, conduct these computer sessions immediately before Investigation 2.

If you have fewer than five computers, immediately after you have introduced the On-Computer Activity, Sunken Ships, in Session 3, assign some students to begin cycling through the computer activity. Make and post a schedule to use during the last four days of the investigation, assigning about 15 to 20 minutes for pairs of students to use the computer(s) throughout the day.

■ Post the *Geo-Logo* User Sheet (p. 149) next to each computer. This sheet provides information about running the program and entering commands, including a picture of the tool bar.

■ If you plan to provide folders in which students will save their work for the entire unit, prepare these for distribution during Session 1.

Coordinates and Distances on a Grid

What Happens

Students learn how to label points on a coordinate grid with an ordered pair of positive numbers. They choose and describe addresses for their own houses on a grid of streets and avenues. They practice using coordinates by delivering envelopes with partial addresses to people living in Grid City. Students learn the concept of distance on a grid as the length of a "taxicab path." Their work focuses on:

- Determining locations on a map of Grid City
- Using coordinates to name and locate addresses on the Grid City map
- Writing coordinates as mathematicians do—that is, with horizontal coordinate first
- Finding "taxicab" distances between two points on a grid

The chart below shows how students work during this session.

Session 1	
Whole Class *40 min.*	**Creating Addresses in Grid City** **Delivering Mail in Grid City** **Reading and Writing Coordinates as Mathematicians Do** **Taxicab Paths in Grid City**
Pairs *20 min.*	**Finding Distances in Grid City**

Materials

- Student Sheet 1 (1 per student, and 1 transparency)
- Student Sheet 2 (1 per pair)
- Student Sheet 3 (1 per student, homework)
- Transparency of Envelopes
- Family letter (1 per student)
- Overhead projector
- Colored pens for the overhead transparencies

Activity

Creating Addresses in Grid City

Show the Grid City map (Student Sheet 1) on a transparency.

Pretend we all moved to Grid City. Here is a map of the city, with a school, a swimming pool, and each of your houses. In Grid City, each building is at a corner, or intersection, of two roads. One road is a street [*indicate the streets along the horizontal axis*] **and one road is an avenue** [*indicate the avenues along the vertical axis*].

Each of you has to choose a house. I'll label that house with your initials.

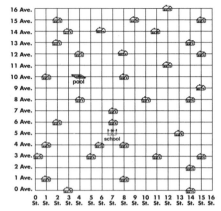

Ask two to four student volunteers to choose a house and tell you which one it is. Let the students figure out how they might do this without pointing (you may want to face the screen so students have to use words).

As each student properly locates a house, write the student's initials near that house. The usefulness of having a standard way to refer to the addresses (by convention, a number for the street followed by a number for the avenues) should emerge from this discussion.

Give students copies of the Grid City map on Student Sheet 1. Have them find and label the houses that have already been chosen. Ask the rest of the students to choose a house by giving the two-number address (for example, "Eighth Street and First Avenue"). After each student states an address, all students write on their sheets that student's initials next to the corresponding house while you label your map on the overhead. If there are more students than houses, students can draw a new house at each location the final students choose.

Activity

Delivering Mail in Grid City

Show the transparency of Envelopes (p. 148), or draw the envelopes on the chalkboard.

The mail carrier in Grid City has several envelopes that have been smudged. Can you help fill in the missing information? For example, on the first envelope, can you tell whose initials have been smudged?

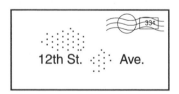

Look at the second envelope. What can you figure out about where this envelope should go? What, then, could the missing information be? Are there any other possibilities?

The rest of the sheet contains envelopes with no address and no initials. Use these for students to make up smudged envelopes to challenge one another. For the first few envelopes, have one student suggest what to fill in for two of the three pieces of missing information—initials, street number, and avenue number—and write these on the overhead or on the board. Then have the rest of the class identify the missing third piece of information.

For the last few envelopes, ask a student to suggest what to fill in for only one of the three pieces of information. Ask the other students to fill in the other two missing pieces. Is there more than one possibility? How do you know?

Reading and Writing Coordinates as Mathematicians Do

The Grid City mail carrier was told to deliver an interesting-looking package to 8th and 10th. Whose house should that package be delivered to?

Accept a few responses from students, enough to indicate that the phrase "8th and 10th" could be interpreted in more than one way, as either 8th Street and 10th Avenue or 8th Avenue and 10th Street. Tell students that the mail carriers decided to adopt the rule that mathematicians use when they are locating a particular point on a grid like this one. They decided always to say the street (along the horizontal) first and the avenue (along the vertical) second. Therefore, "8th and 10th" means 8th Street and 10th Avenue.

Who lives at 8th and 10th? At 10th and 8th?

Suggest a few other locations and have students show the locations on the overhead of Grid City. When students are comfortable locating houses on the grid this way, introduce the written notation for labeling coordinates.

When mathematicians are locating points on a grid, they write down the numbers like this: (8, 10) [*write the ordered pair of numbers on the board*]. This notation for writing two numbers in a specific order is called an *ordered pair*. The numbers in the ordered pair are called the *coordinates* of the point.

Coordinates give an exact location of a point. The first coordinate, or number in the ordered pair, is always on the horizontal number line going from left to right. The second coordinate, or number in the ordered pair, is always on the vertical number line.

Let's try a few.

Write down the coordinates of each house on the grid so students can see how the written notation corresponds to the location of the points on the grid. You may want to have students come up to the overhead of Grid City and show how they find particular points. Give a few clues, such as the following:

Who lives at (4, 8)? How do you know? Where is DK's [*substitute the initials of someone in your class*] house? Where would a house be whose coordinates are (0, 6)?

Then have students take turns giving clues to the rest of the class. When students seem comfortable with locating points on the grid, point to a house and have them write the coordinates. Use the word *coordinates* naturally as it fits into this and subsequent sessions so students will begin to use it appropriately.

Taxicab Paths in Grid City

Show the Grid City map transparency.

Pretend you drive a taxicab in Grid City. You can drive your taxi only along the lines representing the streets and the avenues, not across the squares between the lines. Also, you cannot drive along the same line more than once, since the passenger would have to pay double. Let's see how far it is by taxi from the school to the swimming pool. We'll call the distance between two points on the grid a "block." How many blocks does the taxi have to drive from the school to the swimming pool?

Some students may have trouble understanding the unit of measurement used here. A few may start out counting intersections rather than blocks, arriving at an answer that is one greater than the number of blocks. See the **Teacher Note**, What Are We Measuring? (p. 10), for ways to help students focus on blocks.

Have a student choose one path from the school to the swimming pool and give the coordinates of each intersection as you draw his or her path on the overhead. Count the blocks the taxi traveled and record the number on the board.

Are there other paths the taxi could follow?

Students show different paths between the two points representing the school and the swimming pool. Be sure not to allow paths that go over the same block more than once. Using a different color for each path, draw each path on the overhead. Record the path lengths on the board. After students have offered two or three paths, ask them to consider the shortest path.

Now try to find the shortest path from the school to the swimming pool. Is there more than one shortest path?

The goal of this discussion is to reinforce the definition of distances on the grid and to come to the conclusion that there are many shortest paths between two points.

A final question you may want to ask about this journey is this:

What if the taxi starts at the swimming pool rather than at the school? What is the shortest path? Is it the same length as the path from the school to the swimming pool.

Pairs work together on the Grid City maps (Student Sheet 1), answering the questions on Student Sheet 2, Finding Distances in Grid City. When they are finished, briefly discuss their answers to be sure the concept of distance is clear. Students will do more work with distances on the grid in the next session.

Finding Distances in Grid City

Session 1 Follow-Up

Coordinate Mystery   Send home the family letter or the *Investigations* at Home booklet, along with a copy of Student Sheet 3, Coordinate Mystery. Students complete the picture at home.

 **Homework**

Up until now, students have focused on measuring distances along vertical and horizontal lines on the grid. Drawing the Coordinate Mystery picture requires drawing lines diagonally across squares. Let students know that on this student sheet, and when they make up their own coordinate mysteries, they can draw lines that are not on grid lines.

In this session, we are measuring distances—the number of blocks, or line segments, along the path.

Here the path between the two houses is 6 blocks long.

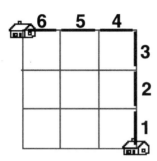

Some students, though, may initially think of a "block" as a square region.

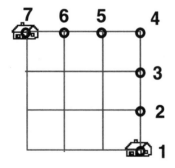

Others may count "blocks" by counting each point, or intersection, with the starting point counted as "1."

You may find that having students think in terms of motion, visualizing themselves walking along the roads in the diagram, helps them think about the problem in ways consistent with our definition of "block." You may want some students to act out being a taxi, counting blocks as they drive along streets and avenues.

Introducing Negative Coordinates

What Happens

Students work with a map of Four-Quadrant City, whose street addresses require negative coordinates. They play Tic-Tac-Toe on the grid to practice using coordinates containing negative numbers. They make up Coordinate Mystery Pictures with negative coordinates and exchange them with other students. Their work focuses on:

- Using negative as well as positive coordinates to find and name locations on a map
- Referring to points by the quadrant in which they lie

The chart below shows how students work during this session.

Session 2	
Whole Class *30 min.*	**Using Negative Coordinates** **Playing Grid Tic-Tac-Toe** (Introduction)
Pairs *30 min.*	**Playing Grid Tic-Tac-Toe** **Coordinate Mystery Pictures**

Materials

- Student Sheet 4 (1 per student, and 1 transparency)
- Student Sheet 5 (3–4 per pair, 1 for homework, and 1 transparency—optional)
- Overhead projector

Activity

Show a transparency of Student Sheet 4, Four-Quadrant City Map.

Here is a map of a neighboring city to Grid City called Four-Quadrant City. When people built this city, they decided to number the streets from the middle of the city rather than from the edge of the city as in Grid City. The Four-Quadrant City post office had to come up with a new way to deliver mail since the way the Grid City post office did it would not work. How do you think the post office decided people should address letters in Four-Quadrant City? Let's find out by starting with some of these people [*indicate Quadrant I*].

What are the addresses for *XY*, *LM*, and *AB*?

Label the positive avenues (vertically up from 0) and the positive streets (from 0 to the right) to help students name the addresses.

Using Negative Coordinates

What address do you think *ZA* should have?

Have students suggest various ideas. See the **Dialogue Box**, Communicating with Negative Numbers (p. 16), for examples of ideas students have come up with.

If your students worked with negative numbers in the third grade units, *Changes Over Time* and *Landmarks in the Hundreds*, or in the fourth grade units, *Mathematical Thinking at Grade 4* and *Landmarks in the Thousands*, the idea of negative numbers will probably come up naturally. If they have not had much experience with negative numbers, you may need to spend extra time on the concept.

You might start like this:

If we think of this [*point to the x-axis*] as a number line, then the numbers to the left of 0 are negative numbers. Similarly, if we also think of this [*point to the y-axis*] as a number line, then the numbers going down from 0 are negative numbers.

State that all the ideas students suggested could be tried, but that negative numbers is the convention used by mathematicians, so we adopt it.

Count on the *x*-axis to the left, continuing past zero to the negative numbers; point to each intersection as you count, saying, . . . **zero, negative one, negative two, negative three.** . . .

How are the addresses of *ZA* and *AB* similar and different? What is the address of *YB*?

Challenge students to give the addresses of *UV* and *GH*, then of *DC* and *CB* (each of which has two negative coordinates).

Continue the discussion by explaining the convention for writing negative coordinates.

Mathematicians use a convention to name negative numbers. They put a minus sign in front of the number. A pair of coordinates with one negative and one positive number looks like this: (–5, 7) or (4, –9) [*write the number pairs on the board*]. A pair of coordinates with two negative numbers looks like this: (–2, –3) [*write the number pair on the board*].

Naming the Quadrants Tell students the names of the four quadrants of the grid so they can use the names when talking about Four-Quadrant City.

Do you have any idea why this city is called Four-Quadrant City? A quadrant is an area or a region. Mathematicians use the word *quadrant* to talk about each of the four areas of the grid. Quadrant I is the one where all the coordinates are positive. Grid City was built just in Quadrant I.

Point out and name the other three quadrants. Show students how the quadrants are named in order counterclockwise (if they are familiar with this term), as shown below. Also tell them it is a convention to refer to quadrants in Roman numerals, as shown here.

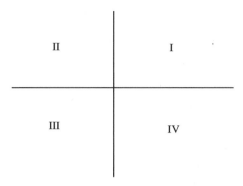

You may want to leave on the board a small drawing of a set of axes with the quadrants labeled. Students will see these quadrant labels many more times in their math careers; the most important thing for them to remember now is the difference between the first quadrant—which has all positive coordinates—and the other three.

Give students copies of Student Sheet 4, Four-Quadrant City Map. Point out that there is only one 0 printed at the point where the axes intersect. This is a shorthand for including two 0's, one for each axis. Have them label the streets and avenues in all four quadrants by placing positive and negative integers along the axes.

As a whole class, place a park on the map as specified on Student Sheet 4.

Where could you put a park so it is fewer than four blocks from the school?

Have a few students respond with possible coordinates for the park. On the transparency, draw a small picture of a park or write the word *park* where students suggest it be located. Have students draw the new addition on their maps.

Students then work in pairs to put a store, a tennis court, a high school, and a video store on the map, as specified on Student Sheet 4. When they are finished, have students describe their locations in terms of coordinates. Show some of the students' solutions on the transparency and discuss them.

Playing Grid Tic-Tac-Toe

Grid Tic-Tac-Toe can be played either on the board or on an overhead. Use a transparency of Student Sheet 5, Grid Paper, or draw a similar grid on the board. Draw a box around nine intersections in a three-by-three arrangement as shown below. This will be the game area. Start with a square in Quadrant I, then move to other quadrants so students must use negative coordinates.

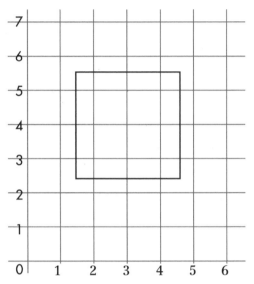

Divide the class into two teams. For each team, choose a spokesperson and a recorder.

In this game, you'll be playing Tic-Tac-Toe by naming the coordinates of the point where you want to put an *X* or an *O*. The object is to get three points in a row.

The first team begins by naming a point by its coordinates. The spokes person is in charge of naming the point, but should consult with other team members. The recorder puts an *X* on the point. (If the spokesperson names a point that is off the game area or is already taken, that team forfeits its turn.) The second team chooses a point and the recorder for that team places an *O* on the point. The teams alternate choosing points. Each time a point is placed on the grid, the recorder starts at the origin and counts off the coordinates (0, 1, 2, 3 or 0, –1, –2, –3)—first in the horizontal direction, then in the vertical direction.

The game ends when one team gets three points in a row. The team that loses starts the next game. If the game is a draw (all nine points are taken, but no team has three in a row), the same team starts the next game.

At some time, you may want to expand the game to four-point Tic-Tac-Toe, in which the game area is four points by four points instead of three by three and teams try to get four points in a row. If you feel your students need more challenge, move on to the four-point game. The strategy for the four-point game is more complex, and the possible points to choose occupy a larger part of the grid.

If there is time after several group games, students can continue to play Grid Tic-Tac-Toe in pairs using copies of Student Sheet 5, Grid Paper.

Activity

Coordinate Mystery Pictures

Briefly discuss the coordinate mystery picture students did for homework (Student Sheet 3). Then tell students they are going to make up their own coordinate mystery pictures using points in all four quadrants. Pass out copies of Student Sheet 5, Grid Paper.

Make up your own coordinate mystery for other people in the class to solve. Use the Grid Paper to draw your picture, then write the coordinates in order on another sheet with your name on it. Your picture must include between six and ten points and must use points in all four quadrants. When you are finished, bring me your list of coordinates and I will arrange a trade. You may want to look at the coordinate mystery you solved last night to remember how to make a mystery picture.

As students bring their finished coordinate mysteries to you, look over them quickly to see if you can find any obvious errors (for example, coordinates larger than 10 or smaller than –10). Trade each mystery with the next student who arrives with a completed page.

Students can make and exchange coordinate mysteries in class or at home throughout the rest of this investigation. They are good practice for working with coordinates and a good way to get families involved in this unit.

Session 2 Follow-Up

Coordinate Mystery Picture or Grid Tic-Tac-Toe   To give students more practice with negative coordinates, for homework they can either make another coordinate mystery picture at home to exchange with a friend in class tomorrow or play Grid Tic-Tac-Toe with someone at home. In either case, they will need another copy of Student Sheet 5, Grid Paper.

 **Homework**

Communicating with Negative Numbers

This discussion takes place while students are working on the activity Using Negative Coordinates (p. 11).

What address do you think *ZA* should have?

Kim: (1, 4).

What address does *AB* have?

The class: (1, 4).

So where should the mail carrier take a letter addressed (1, 4)?

Kenyana: We should use alphabet letters for that side of the city.

Joey: No! Just reverse the coordinates! Say (4, 1) instead of (1, 4).

Sarah: That wouldn't work! What about the (4, 1) over on the east!

Rafael: I think, if you were counting, 8, 7, 6, 5, 4, 3, 2, 1, 0, then minus 1, minus 2. . . .

So, use negative numbers?

Rafael: Yes. Just go the other way.

Later, the teacher notices that some students sometimes drop the word *negative*. She decides that the best teaching strategy would be to emphasize communication failures this might cause. This happens when Jesse is naming a point to which *UV* could have walked.

Jesse: *UV* could have walked to (2, 3).

[*The teacher purposely begins gesturing to mark the point (2, 3).*]

Jesse: No! Not there!

Oh, what did you say? (2, 3)?

Jesse: Yeah. Oh! (2, –3).

Ah-ha! (2, –3). Now I understand you.

Playing Sunken Ships

What Happens

In Session 3, students discuss how to find all locations a given distance away from a point on the grid. They learn to play Sunken Ships both on and off the computer. Then half the class works in pairs playing Sunken Ships on the computer while the other half works in pairs playing the game off the computer. Halfway through the work period the groups switch.

In Session 4, students again play Sunken Ships both on and off the computer. The off-computer group may also make and exchange coordinate mysteries. In the last 30 minutes, the class figures out how to determine the length of the shortest path from the lower-right corner to the upper-left corner of a grid. Their work focuses on:

■ Combining coordinates and distances on the full grid

■ Identifying areas on the grid as points less than or greater than a particular distance

■ Using distances on a grid to develop strategies in a game

■ Discovering patterns in the lengths of paths in grids

The following charts show how students work during these sessions.

Materials

■ Transparency of Student Sheet 4 (from Session 2)

■ Student Sheet 6 (2 per student)

■ Student Sheet 7 (3–4 per student, and 1 transparency)

■ Student Sheet 8 (1 per pair)

■ Student Sheet 9 (1 per student, and 1 transparency)

■ *Geo-Logo* User Sheet (1 per computer)

■ Overhead projector

■ Computers with *Geo-Logo* installed

■ Colored pens for the overhead transparencies

■ Crayons or colored pencils (several per student)

Session 3

Whole Class 30 min.	Introducing Work Procedures	
	Finding All Locations a Given Distance Away	
	Off-Computer Activity: Playing Sunken Ships on Paper (Introduction)	
	On-Computer Activity: Playing Sunken Ships on the Computer (Introduction)	
Two Groups (working in pairs) 15 min.	Group A On-Computer Activity ■ Playing Sunken Ships on the Computer	Group B Off-Computer Activity ■ Playing Sunken Ships on Paper
Switch 15 min.	Off-Computer Activity ■ Playing Sunken Ships on Paper	On-Computer Activity ■ Playing Sunken Ships on the Computer
Teacher Check-point	Students' Use of Coordinates and Distances	

Session 4

Two Groups (working in pairs) 15 min.	Group A On-Computer Activity ■ Playing Sunken Ships on the Computer	Group B Off-Computer Activity ■ Playing Sunken Ships on Paper
Switch 15 min.	Off-Computer Activity ■ Playing Sunken Ships on Paper	On-Computer Activity ■ Playing Sunken Ships on the Computer
Teacher Check-point	Students' Use of Coordinates and Distances	
Whole Class 30 min.	Discussing Sunken Ships Strategies	
	Shortest Paths on a Grid	

Tell students that today they will be using computers. Based on how you have structured your class, explain how the class will operate during the remainder of the unit so everyone has an opportunity to do the computer work. See Managing the Computer Activities in This Unit (p. I-19).

For example, you might state that:

■ each day the class work time will be divided into two equal periods.

■ half the students will work on the computer during the first period of time, with the rest of the students working at their seats; then the groups will switch.

■ students are to work with the same partner(s) for the entire unit.

■ students are to save their work on a disk (or are to use the same computer throughout the unit).

■ when working at computers, partners are to take turns, with one person using the mouse and the keyboard and the other doing the reading and writing. They are to trade places after a period of time—for example, every 5 minutes.

Explain that at the beginning of each class session, you will introduce the On-Computer Activity and/or the Off-Computer Activity.

Show the transparency of the Four-Quadrant City Map (Student Sheet 4) on the overhead projector.

On a shopping trip, *AB*, who lives at (1, 4), walks exactly 2 blocks away from his home, then can't remember how to get home. He calls a friend for help. She offers to meet him, but all he can tell her is that he is 2 blocks from home. Where are all the intersections where *AB* might be standing?

Give students time to figure out the intersections. Then mark the intersections they identify on the transparency. Ask them the following:

How did you find the intersection you named?

How do you know when you have found all the intersections?

Do you see any pattern to these points?

Do another problem like the one above, where the starting point is not in Quadrant I. Students should notice that the solutions lie on the sides of a square that is tilted.

Off-Computer Activity: Playing Sunken Ships on Paper

In the following activities, students will be playing Sunken Ships in teams of 2 (with a few teams of 3 if there is an odd number of students) both on and off the computer.

We're going to play Sunken Ships, a game in which your team must locate a sunken ship. A long time ago, a pirate ship containing many treasures sank to the bottom of the sea. You are part of a team of scientists searching for it. Your boat has a special tool that can tell if there is part of a ship directly underneath. Your job is to move your boat to grid locations on the surface of the ocean and beam down to see if you can find the sunken ship by locating 5 points on the ship. If there is part of a ship underneath your grid location, the computer or the other team will tell you. You will be playing the game both on and off the computer.

To play the game on paper, one team draws a sunken ship on the grid without letting the other team see the location of the ship. The ship must cover 5 consecutive intersections lying on a vertical or horizontal straight line. The other team must guess all 5 intersections of the ship on the grid.

Using the top grid on a transparency of Student Sheet 7, Sunken Ships Grids, demonstrate drawing the ship.

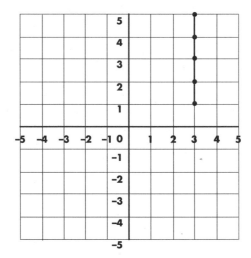

Of course, ships at sea are not located with streets and avenues. But scientists do use coordinates on grids to determine the locations of ships.

While you are talking about the Sunken Ship game, you can introduce the words *x-axis* (the horizontal axis), *y-axis* (the vertical axis), *x-coordinate* (the number of units from 0 along the *x*-axis), and *y-coordinate* (the number of units from 0 along the *y*-axis). Use these words and explain their meanings as they come up naturally. Do not insist that students use these terms.

Using the ship you have drawn on the transparency, demonstrate how to determine how far away a guessed point is from the ship. Remind students that in determining distance, they are counting blocks not intersections. In this case, you may want to call the blocks "units" rather than "blocks" because the grid represents the ocean bottom rather than city blocks. Write the distance for some guessed points on the grid, as shown. Remind students that their guess is measured from the closest unlocated point on the ship. This point may change from one turn to the next, depending on the location of their guess.

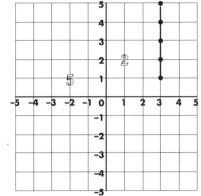

Now play a demonstration game using the bottom grid on the transparency. The rules for Sunken Ships are specified in detail on Student Sheet 6, How to Play Sunken Ships on Paper. It is a good idea to have students read them with you.

- Decide on 5 points that represent your ship.

- Have students guess points on the grid.

- Tell students how many units away each guess is from the nearest unlocated point on the ship.

- Mark their guesses on the transparency. If the point is on the ship, put an *S* (for ship) on the point. If the point is not on the ship, write the distance it is from the closest point on the ship.

- Continue playing the game until the class locates all 5 points of your ship.

- Count the number of guesses it took.

You will all have an opportunity to play Sunken Ships today. Remember when you play to be careful that you always measure the distance from the *closest point on the ship that has not yet been located*. Also, be sure not to give your opponents wrong information—that will throw them off unfairly. Check your information with your partner before you tell it to the other team.

Activity

On-Computer Activity: Playing Sunken Ships on the Computer

Note: It is critical that you have completed the relevant parts of the *Geo-Logo* Teacher Tutorial (see p. 91) and played a few games of Sunken Ships before you begin this lesson. Post copies of the *Geo-Logo* User Sheet next to each computer.

You can play Sunken Ships against the computer. The rules are the same, but the way you play is just a bit different. The computer hides the ship, and you try to locate it using a new *Geo-Logo* command I will teach you.

Gather the students around the computer (preferably one with a large display) so they can all see the screen. Demonstrate how to:

- turn on the computer
- open *Geo-Logo*
- open Sunken Ships

Explain the Sunken Ships instructions.

Geo-Logo has hidden a ship covering five intersections. You must find the Sunken Ship by locating its five points on the grid. To begin, press the `<return>` key to close the instruction box.

Note: To make commands easier for the students to read while you are demonstrating computer activities, increase the font size by choosing **All Large** on the **Font** menu. (When you are finished demonstrating, remember to return the font to its regular size by choosing **All Small** on the **Font** menu.)

Type `hideship` and press the `<return>` key.

To find the ship on the computer, you specify coordinates in a slightly different way than you do when playing the paper version of Sunken Ships. You still use coordinates, but you guess them by using a command that tells the turtle to "jump to" a particular location. For example, `jumpto [1 1]` tells the turtle to "jump to the position at coordinates (1, 1)." Before you type `jumpto`, be sure the cursor is in the Command Center.

The instructions for playing the game on the computer are on Student Sheet 8, How to Play Sunken Ships on the Computer.

Type examples of `jumpto` commands and have students predict where the turtle will land (by pointing to the screen). Then press `<return>` to see if the turtle lands where the students thought it would.

Something you must remember about the `jumpto` command is that *Geo-Logo* uses a different convention to write coordinates than we use on paper. *Geo-Logo* uses square brackets instead of parentheses and it does not need a comma between the two numbers.

See the **Teacher Note**, Notational Conventions in *Geo-Logo* (p. 27).

Now play a game of Sunken Ships on the computer. (Click the **Erase All tool** and retype `hideship` before you start the game to get rid of any commands you typed.)

Have students suggest where to jump to.

Notice that *Geo-Logo* prints the distance clues and *S*'s (for ship) on the grid, just as you do when you play the game on paper. It also prints the coordinates you guessed and the results of each guess in the Print window for easy reference.

You win the game when you find all 5 points and the sunken ship appears. Try to win with as few `jumpto` commands as you can by using mathematical strategies. For each game, keep track of the number of `jumpto` commands you use on the bottom of Student Sheet 8, How to Play Sunken Ships on the Computer.

To play another game, click the Erase All tool, type `hideship`, and press **<return>** to get a ship at a different location.

Classroom Management

Divide the class into two groups. Assign one group to work with partners on the Off-Computer Activity and the other group to work with partners on the On-Computer Activity. Switch groups halfway through the work period. This organization is for the second half of Session 3 and the first half of Session 4.

Off the computer, one pair plays Sunken Ships against another pair. They use Student Sheet 6, How to Play Sunken Ships on Paper, for instructions, and copies of Student Sheet 7, Sunken Ships Grids, to play the game. *On the computer*, pairs play Sunken Ships. They use Student Sheet 8, How to Play Sunken Ships on the Computer, for instructions. You may want to give them copies of Student Sheet 7, Sunken Ships Grids, to keep track of how far their guesses are from the ship.

Teacher Checkpoint

Students' Use of Coordinates and Distances

While students are playing Sunken Ships in Sessions 3 and 4 on and off the computer, watch to see if they are proficient with coordinates and distances on the grid. Notice the following:

- Do they name locations confidently and consistently?
- Are they sure about the order of coordinates?
- Can they locate negative coordinates as easily as positive coordinates?
- Do they count "units" when they are calculating distance, or do they sometimes count intersections?
- Are distances between negative coordinates problematic?
- Are they using the distance clues to help make their next guess?

If any of these issues is a consistent problem for several students, you may want to call the class together before you switch groups and give a short review.

Discussing Sunken Ships Strategies

After every student has had an opportunity to play Sunken Ships on the computer at least twice and off the computer at least twice, hold a brief discussion about the strategies they used to find the ship:

- Did they have a strategy for deciding where to make their first guess?
- Did they draw anything on their grid when they got a response to a guess?
- How did they choose the next point to guess?

Ask students to describe the strategies they used. If they have trouble, play a game with the class in which students describe how they are thinking about their guesses.

Students might use what they know about distances on grids to help them play the game. One clue they can use is the number they record for the misses. For example, suppose a student guessed (–2, 2) and was told it missed by 5. The student can draw all the possible points 5 units from (–2, 2). The result is part of a tilted square, as shown here.

This part of a square was drawn after the point (–2, 2) was said to "miss by 5." It indicates that (a) one location must lie on a point the segments pass through and (b) no undiscovered point on the ship lies inside the square.

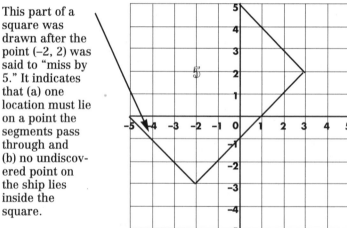

The strategy of drawing part of the tilted square provides a lot of guidance for the next guess. See the **Dialogue Box**, Guessing Smart with Mathematical Thinking (p. 28), for an example of how to use this information.

If you would like to discuss this strategy with your class, show the transparency of Student Sheet 7, Sunken Ships Grids, again, and give a copy of the sheet to each student. Use the top grid and refer to the points you have marked there.

Suppose Team 1 drew a ship on the grid and Team 2 asked if the ship was on the point (1, 0). Team 1 said, "Missed the closest point on our ship by 3 units."

What are all the possible locations for the closest point on the ship?

Students work in small groups on their copies of Student Sheet 7 to find all possible locations of the closest point on the ship.

Illustrate the situation on the transparency. The *x*'s are all points that are 3 away from the guessed point.

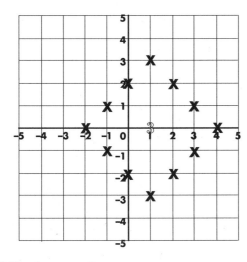

Note: If one or more points on a ship have been identified, the diamond shape will indicate all the possible locations for the closest *undiscovered* point on the ship.

Discuss the following questions:

What spatial pattern can you find? (a diamond shape)

At what points on the grid do you know there can't be any points on the ship? (inside the diamond)

If a player guessed point (–3, 1) and missed the ship by 4 units, what would all the possible locations of the closest undiscovered point on the ship be?

Have the whole class discuss its findings. Then ask students to predict the locations for 5 units away from some point not in the first quadrant.

Activity

Shortest Paths on a Grid

If your class has time, you can use the following activity to connect thinking about distances on grids with number patterns.

Now that you have played Sunken Ships and worked with paths on a grid, we're going to explore patterns in paths on some simple grids.

Show Student Sheet 9, Patterns in Paths, on an overhead transparency. Give each student a copy of Student Sheet 9.

Ask students about the 2 by 2 grid in the upper left of the sheet.

How many blocks is the shortest path from the bottom-right corner to the upper-left corner?

Are there several paths that are this length?

What are they?

Use different colors to trace a few paths on the grid. When students agree they have found the length of the shortest path, fill in the table at the right side of the transparency with the length of the path.

Fill in the next few lines of this table by figuring out the length of the shortest path from the bottom right to the top left of each grid on the sheet. Use different-colored pencils or crayons if you want to look at more than one path on a grid.

See if you can find a pattern so that you could know the length of the shortest path for any square grid without drawing the path. Use that pattern to fill in the path length for the larger grids in your table—for example, the one with 50 rows and 50 columns.

The second part of the exploration is looking at grids that are rectangles but not squares. These grids have a different number of rows and columns.

First find the length of the shortest path on the grids on the sheet. Then see if you can find a pattern that helps you fill in the rest of the table.

Working in pairs, students begin working on these sheets in class. They finish them for homework.

Sessions 3 and 4 Follow-Up

 **Homework**

Sunken Ships   After Session 3, each student teaches Sunken Ships to someone at home and plays several games with that person. Students will need several copies of Student Sheet 7, Sunken Ships Grids, and a copy of Student Sheet 6, How to Play Sunken Ships on Paper.

Patterns in Paths   After Session 4, students finish Student Sheet 9, Patterns in Paths, for homework if they did not finish it in class.

 **Extension**

More Sunken Ships   Students can play a more difficult version of Sunken Ships off the computer by hiding three ships. One ship is three points long, one is four, and one is five. The game is played the same way. To win, the student must locate all three ships. Either version of Sunken Ships can be played at other free times or used as a Ten-Minute Math session.

Notational Conventions in Geo-Logo

Help students understand that the conventions used to specify coordinates in traditional mathematical notation and in *Geo-Logo* notation are different:

In mathematics we use parentheses and a comma between the numbers: (–20, 60)

In *Geo-Logo* we use square brackets and no comma between the numbers: [–20 60] Parentheses and commas have been reserved for a different meaning in *Geo-Logo* and so can not be used in this case.

The `jumpto` command uses square brackets instead of parentheses and doesn't require a comma between the coordinates. (*Geo-Logo* will accept notation with or without a comma.)

You might want to discuss with students that many conventions in mathematics and computer programming are arbitrary. They're only "right" because people have agreed to do things that way for consistency.

Challenge students to differentiate by example between facts in mathematics that must be so— such as, 3 + 4 is equal to 7, and that the point (3, 4) lies between the points (2, 4) and (4, 4)— and "facts" that are so just because they are agreed-on conventions—such as, the symbol + means *add*, and the *x*-coordinate comes before the *y*-coordinate in naming coordinates.

DIALOGUE BOX

Guessing Smart with Mathematical Thinking

This class was just starting to play Sunken Ships on paper. The teacher thought that playing the game once as a group might encourage students to think about good guessing strategies.

The teacher recorded her ship's location on a paper hidden next to the overhead projector, showed the blank Sunken Ships transparency to the class, then challenged the class:

You'll never find my ship!

Because any guess would be a good start, the teacher began by calling on a student who was not very confident with coordinates.

Marci: I guess (5, –4).

The teacher marked that point (see grid 1), checked the hidden ship, and announced:

That is 9 units away from the nearest possible location on my ship! Think before you guess again—would (4, –4) be a smart next guess?

Grid 1

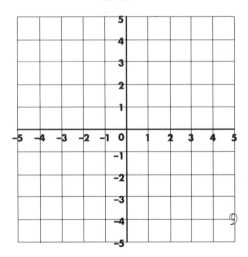

To the teacher's surprise, the class gave derisive hoots!

Irena: That would be dumb! The ship couldn't be less than 9 units away.

B. J.: Yeah. Try something else, like (0, 0).

The teacher marked that point (see grid 2).

Grid 2

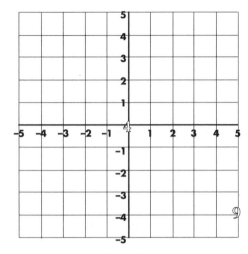

That is 4 units away from the nearest possible location on the ship. Tell me what else you know. What would be a smart next guess?

Students talked in small groups of three or four deciding what they would propose. One group conversation went as follows:

Alex: Let's find all the points it could be.

Lesley Ann: Yes! All the points 4 away from (0, 0). It will be a tilted square, just like we found before.

They began to plot every one of these points when the teacher interrupted.

Not the full square. Some of them wouldn't be nine away from (5, –4). And they have to be.

The group excitedly gave their next guess.

Group: We say (1, 1).

Continued on next page

The teacher marked that location (see grid 3).

Grid 3

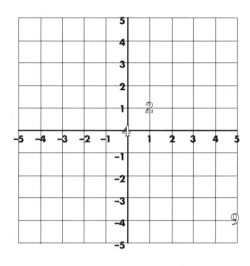

That's 2 units away.

Joey: Then (2, 2) because it's got to be farther away from the 4. That's got to be it!

You found a point on my ship! (see grid 4)

Grid 4

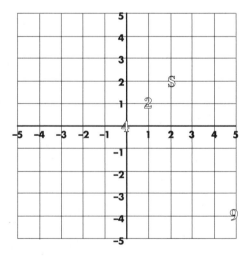

Distances On and Off the Computer

Materials

- Student Sheet 10
  (1 per pair, and 1
  transparency)
- Student Sheet 11
  (1 per pair)
- Student Sheet 12
  (1 per student)
- Student Sheet 13
  (1 per student)
- Overhead projector
- Computers

What Happens

Students learn how to use *Geo-Logo* to draw paths on a grid. They use the On-Computer Activity, Taxi, to find the shortest path that reaches five different houses and returns home. Off computer, they explore how to find the distance between two points on the grid from the coordinates of the points. In Session 6, the entire class does the Assessment: Designing a Town during their off-computer time. Students' work focuses on:

- Using *Geo-Logo* to specify motions on a grid
- Organizing an investigation to find the shortest of several possible paths
- Using coordinate values as information in finding the distance between two points
- Satisfying complex constraints in locating points on a grid

The following charts show how students work during these sessions.

Session 5		
Whole Class *30 min.*	**Discussing Shortest Paths** **Introducing *Geo-Logo* Movement Commands** **On-Computer Activity: Taxi** (Introduction)	
Two Groups (working in pairs) *15 min.*	Group A **On-Computer Activity** ■ Taxi	Group B **Off-Computer Activity** ■ Distances and Coordinates
Switch *15 min.*	**Off-Computer Activity** ■ Distances and Coordinates	**On-Computer Activity** ■ Taxi

Session 6	
Whole Class *15 min.*	**Using Coordinates to Find Distances**

	Group A	Group B
Two Groups (working in pairs) *15 min.*	**On-Computer Activity** ■ Taxi	**Off-Computer Activity** ■ Distances and Coordinates
Switch *15 min.*	**Off-Computer Activity** ■ Distances and Coordinates	**On-Computer Activity** ■ Taxi
Indivi–duals *15 min.*	**Assessment: Designing a Town** (done during off-computer time)	

 Ten-Minute Math: Lengths and Perimeters Note: The repeat command is not presented until later in this unit, although it is available for students to use on the computer anytime. If your students have not used the repeat command, you will need to introduce it the first time you do this activity. For hints, see the complete directions for Ten-Minute Math (p. 87).

A few times during the next few days, do Lengths and Perimeters (off-computer problems with the *Geo-Logo* repeat command). Remember, Ten-Minute Math activities are done outside of math time during any spare ten minutes you have during the day, perhaps right before lunch or at the end of the day.

Choose a distance you want the turtle to go, for instance 40. Ask students to work in pairs for two to three minutes to write down as many repeat commands as they can think of that would move the turtle that distance. They use the format repeat __ [fd __]. They can use calculators to test their ideas.

Make a list on the board or on an overhead transparency of all the different responses.

Ask students to prove that their responses work:

How do you know repeat 2 [fd 20] would be 40 turtle steps?

Discuss whether they have all the possibilities:

Do we have all the repeat commands that work? How do you know? Could we do anything with repeat 8? Could we do anything using fd 11?

For variations on this activity, see p. 87.

Activity

Discussing Shortest Paths

Before you begin working with the computer, discuss students' work on Student Sheet 9, Patterns in Paths.

What patterns did you find for the length of the shortest path in a square grid?

How long would the path be in a grid with 100 rows and 100 columns? 200 rows and 200 columns?

Does the pattern keep working no matter how big the grid gets?

Continue the discussion with questions concerning rectangles:

What pattern did you find for the length of the shortest path in a rectangular grid?

Is it really a different pattern from the one for a square grid?

How long would the shortest path be for a grid with 100 rows and 200 columns?

Does this pattern keep working no matter how big the grid gets?

The **Dialogue Box**, Patterns, Predictions, and Reasons (p. 41), describes the kinds of responses students may give to these questions.

Activity

Introducing *Geo-Logo* Movement Commands

This is a variant of the introductory activity students do in third grade to learn how to use *Geo-Logo*. It introduces the movement commands forward (fd), backward (bk), right turn (rt), and left turn (lt). Do as much of the introductory activities as you think necessary for your students. If the students are familiar with *Geo-Logo*, you can proceed immediately to the Taxi activity.

We are going to write commands that will give directions for someone, or a robot, to walk a path. The commands tell the person to move or

turn. The move commands are "forward" and "back"[*write* fd and bk *on the board or a chart*] and the turn commands are "right" and "left" [*write* rt *and* lt *on the board or a chart*]. Each command is followed by a number that tells how far to move, for fd and bk, or how much to turn, for rt and lt.

Ask a student to come to the front to serve as a robot. Then say:

For example, if I want a robot to walk 5 steps forward, I would write fd 5.

Have the "robot" demonstrate the movement while you write the command on the board.

Now if I want our robot to turn and face the windows [*select something in the room that is 90° to the right of the robot*], **I would write** rt 90.

Again, have the "robot" demonstrate the turn while you write the command on the board under the first command.

A 90-degree (90°) turn is like commands given to bands marching in a parade or like turning from 12 to 3 on a clock.

Write the command fd 5 on the board under the first two commands and ask the robot to follow it. (There should be three commands on the board: fd 5, rt 90, and fd 5.)

Ask another student to come to the board and draw the path the robot

walked—for example, ⌐ .

Tell the students that they will play a game during which they will design a path for a robot, write commands for the path, and see if a robot can follow the commands. This path can be composed of no more than five straight line segments and can have only 90° turns or square corners (like the path just drawn on the board).

Identify a robot and an assistant and have them leave the room. Ask someone to draw a path on the board following the rules above. Ask the class to identify a series of commands that will teach the robot how to walk a similar path. Record the commands on the board. Hide the path by taping paper over it and have the robot and assistant return.

Read the commands and ask the robot to walk the path, with help from the assistant, who monitors which command is next. The class should note any problems and possible reasons for them. Ask the robot and the assistant to draw the path the robot actually walked on the chalkboard while the rest of the students draw it at their seats. Then compare the drawings to the original path and discuss any discrepancies.

Repeat the activity with a new robot and assistant, possibly with some closed paths to check if the robot ends up where he or she started.

On-Computer Activity: Taxi

Note: It is critical that you complete the *Geo-Logo* Teacher Tutorial (p. 91) and do the On-Computer Activity, Taxi, yourself before starting the On-Computer Activity with students. Post copies of the *Geo-Logo* User Sheet next to each computer.

You may want to read the **Teacher Note**, Thinking Geometrically with *Geo-Logo* (p. 39), before starting this session. It provides a perspective for thinking about students' use of *Geo-Logo* in this activity and the rest of the investigation.

Today, you're going to drive a turtle taxi through roads on a grid map. In this activity, called Taxi, there are five houses to which you have to make a delivery. Your job is to find the shortest way you can drive the taxi to each house, then return to the beginning.

The commands you are going to use to drive the taxi are fd, bk, lt, and rt. Because taxi steps are very small, you will be using numbers like 10 and 50 to tell the taxi how far to go.

Gather students around the computer, preferably one with a large display so they can all see the screen. Demonstrate how to:

- turn on the computer
- open *Geo-Logo*
- open Taxi

Explain the Taxi directions:

You must teach the taxi to drive along the shortest path that goes to each of the five houses to make deliveries and back to the beginning.

Note: To make the commands easier for the students to see while you are demonstrating computer activities, increase the font size by choosing **All Large** on the **Font** menu. (When you are finished demonstrating, remember to return the font to its regular size by choosing **All Small** on the **Font** menu.)

To begin, I press the <return> key to close the instruction box.

Now I type map and press the <return> key. A grid map with five houses appears.

Remind students that the four basic *Geo-Logo* commands are fd, bk, rt 90, and lt 90, and tell them they are posted on a *Geo-Logo* User Sheet beside each computer.

During the demonstration, put a transparency of Student Sheet 10, Taxi, on the overhead.

Explain that on the map the turtle's belly is right at an intersection and that the blocks are 10 turtle steps each.

Students suggest what commands to type for the turtle to get to a house. Type the commands as they are suggested by the students without evaluating them in any way. As you type them, announce every key you press. For example:

We want to go forward 20 turtle steps, so I'll type fd **<space>** 20, **then press the <return> key. A space separates the command and the number.**

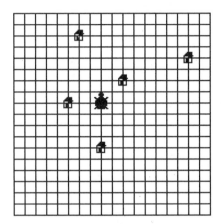

Sometimes when entering commands, pretend to "forget" to enter **<return>** until the class reminds you to do so. Also, make a typing mistake and show how the **<delete>** key can be used to erase typing mistakes.

Show how commands can be edited, such as changing an fd 20 to an fd 40.

I can change anything I have already typed. I use the mouse or the arrow keys to move the cursor in the Command Center right after the 20, press the <delete> key two times to remove the 20, and type 40. When I press <return> I see the effect of that change—the turtle runs the new commands and so now the line segment is 40 turtle steps long.

Using the Tools Demonstrate how clicking on the **Erase One tool** ![icon] at the top of the screen erases the last command, and how the **Label Lengths tool** ![icon] can help find the total length of the path. Show students how to teach the turtle their solution by choosing the **Teach tool** ![icon], naming their procedure, and running it by entering its name in the Command Center. Then show them how to erase the procedure with the **Erase All tool** ![icon] before beginning a new path. (See p. 124 in the *Geo-Logo* Teacher Tutorial for more information on these tools.) Tell students that to draw a new path, they must retype map and press the **<return>** key.

Pass out a copy of Student Sheet 10, Taxi, to each pair of students. Tell them it includes reminders about the steps they must follow to play Taxi.

Saving Work If students need to leave the computers before they finish the activity, they should save their work on the computer's internal drive or on a disk so they will be able to go on from where they left off.

If you need to leave the computer before you are finished, you will want to save your work. Then you can begin where you left off the next time you use the computer.

Choose Save My Work from the File menu. The computer will ask you for a name for your work. There are three things I want you to include in the name:

- the initials (or first or last names) of you and your partner(s)
- a short one-word name for the activity
- the date

Then tomorrow you will be able to find your work easily.

For example, if Karen Jones and Kyle Cortier are working together, they could name their work "KJ + KC taxi 3/22."

Activity

Off-Computer Activity: Distances and Coordinates

Students who are not working on the computer work on Student Sheet 11, Distances and Coordinates. They figure out the shortest distance between several sets of points given as coordinates. A grid is available for them to plot the points, but some students may be able to figure out the distance by examining the coordinates.

Activity

Using Coordinates to Find Distances

At the beginning of Session 6, have a discussion about the process of finding distances, given coordinates.

Did you find any methods to determine the shortest distance between two points on the grid without drawing the points on the grid and counting them?

Students discuss how they might do this. Some students may have come up with a rule for manipulating the coordinates of the points. See the **Teacher Note**, Finding the Shortest Distance on a Grid (p. 40).

Challenge the class to figure out distances that are off the grid, such as the distance between (1, 130) and (200, 55) without drawing the coordinates and counting them on the grid. Limit your problems to the first quadrant, since working with coordinates gets more complicated in other quadrants.

Assessment

Designing a Town

During Session 6 off-computer time, students work alone on Student Sheet 12, Designing a Town, and Student Sheet 13, Procedure Planning Paper. They place houses, parks, a school, a swimming pool, and stores on a grid map, satisfying a set of constraints. Many possible map configurations fit these constraints. In addition, they write about two of the buildings they locate.

Look at their maps and reasoning, considering the following:

- Can they name points in all four quadrants?
- Can they figure out distances with both negative and positive coordinates?
- Can they figure out which points are more and less than a certain distance apart?
- Can they do arithmetic with distances (for example, add them or subtract them) and interpret the results as distances?
- Can they coordinate measurements to more than one object at once?

❖ **Tip for the Linguistically Diverse Classroom** You may wish to have limited English proficient students do this assessment orally. Read aloud each task on Student Sheet 12, making the directions comprehensible by modeling actions and drawing quick sketches.

Classroom Management

Divide the class into two groups. Assign one group to work in pairs on the On-Computer Activity, Taxi, and the other group to work on the Off-Computer Activity. During Session 5, students not using the computer work in pairs on the Student Sheet 11, Distances and Coordinates. During Session 6, students not working on the computer work individually on Student Sheet 12, Designing a Town. Switch groups between on-computer and off-computer activities halfway through the work period.

While Students Are Working If your students have not used *Geo-Logo* before, you will probably need to spend the major portion of your time helping them get started and enter commands on the computer. When they ask for assistance, answer their questions, and refer them to the *Geo-Logo* User Sheet posted next to the computer.

When a pair finds a solution to Taxi, remind students to teach the turtle the solution by choosing the **Teach tool**. Many students will naturally explore all the tools (pictured in the top tools bar). Any tools that are available for an activity may be useful, and students cannot harm anything by exploring them.

When you feel students are ready, show them how to use the **Help** menu to get information about the tools, as well as about windows, vocabulary, directions, and hints.

When it is near the time to switch groups, remind the students working at the computers how to save their work, either on a disk or on the computer's internal drive. (You may wish to gather them around one computer to see the process again while you demonstrate with one pair's work. Then students can go back and save their own work.) Don't forget to teach the second group of students how to save their work at the end of the session.

Sessions 5 and 6 Follow-Up

 **Extension**

Distances with Negative Coordinates Students can continue to explore their methods for finding the shortest distance between points to see if it works with negative coordinates. For example, Does it work with (–2, 2) and (–4, 7)? How about (2, 2), and (–4, 7)? (–2, 2) and (4, 7)? See the **Teacher Note**, Finding the Shortest Distance on a Grid (p. 40).

Thinking Geometrically with Geo-Logo

Geo-Logo is a special geometry-oriented version of Logo, a well-known computer language used internationally for teaching mathematics. What benefit is there for students in using *Geo-Logo*? In what ways do explorations with *Geo-Logo* help students become more competent in geometric thinking?

One major difference between *Geo-Logo* activities and pencil-and-paper geometry activities is that, in *Geo-Logo*, the emphasis is on constructing geometric paths, figures, and designs rather than on recognizing and naming them, as is often the case in standard curricula. *Geo-Logo* provides an environment in which students can easily create and modify geometric figures. They are engaged in constructing geometric figures using mathematical language.

A second major difference concerns the ways in which students verbalize the actions they perform. *Geo-Logo* requires students to communicate with the turtle in a geometrically oriented language. Thus, in the process of making squares, students see that the sides must be equal lengths because all four commands that draw sides contain the same length.

The *Geo-Logo* language requires students to be precise, differentiating in writing between, for example, an 89-degree angle and a 90-degree one. This precision, which differs significantly from the much looser precision of drawings, also makes it possible to compare two students' drawings of a square. While two hand-drawn squares can look similar, even if the two students have different conceptions of a square, two *Geo-Logo* squares will highlight even small differences between students' procedures for drawing them.

Geo-Logo procedures can be run repeatedly and are guaranteed to produce the same drawing each time (assuming the turtle starts in the same place). Students can actually study what their procedures do by running them one step at a time and fixing individual pieces of them, if necessary.

Finally, computers in general, and *Geo-Logo* in particular, motivate students. The artistic aspect of some activities can provide students with a different approach to geometric concepts.

This information is provided as mathematical background to students' work. It is important that you do not teach these routines to students or even expect that all students will discover these patterns when exploring how distances can be determined from coordinates.

As students have probably noticed, one of the shortest routes between two points in taxicab geometry is along two sides of a rectangle constructed with the two points as two of the corners. To figure out the length of one side of the rectangle, you can subtract the smaller x-coordinate from the larger x-coordinate. To figure out the length of the other side of the rectangle, you subtract the smaller y-coordinate from the larger y-coordinate.

For example, if you are trying to find the shortest route between (5, 2) and (2, 10), subtract the two x-coordinates, 5 minus 2, to get a length of 3 for one side, and subtract the two y-coordinates, 10 minus 2, get a length of 8 for the other side. For these two points, the shortest route is 3 + 8, or 11, blocks long.

If you are taking a different route, but still with no backtracking, between the same points, the route is still 11 blocks long. For example, if you start at (5, 2), move up two units to (5, 4), left two units to (3, 4), up six units to (3, 10), then left one unit to (2, 10), the total distance is the sum of the horizontal and vertical units traveled—in this case 2 + 2 + 6 + 1 = 11.

Notice that here is a case where the order in which the two x-coordinates or two y-coordinates appear in the problem doesn't matter. You always subtract the smaller from the larger. What happens with negative coordinates is somewhat more complicated, although the idea is the same. Try to find some distances that involve negative coordinates, such as the distance between (5, 2) and (–2, 10). How is this different from the previous problem? Can you make a procedure that will work for negative coordinates?

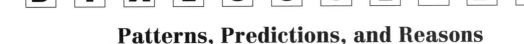

Patterns, Predictions, and Reasons

During the activity, Discussing Shortest Paths (p. 32), the class was discussing the number of blocks in the shortest path for different square grids. The teacher asked the student groups to summarize what they knew.

Marci: The number always goes up by 2.

Alex: It's even numbers.

David: You add 2 each time to the one before.

Karen: It's adding the grid numbers.

What do you mean by that?

Karen: For the 2 by 2, it's 2 plus 2. And it's the same for all of them.

Shoshana: No, we got something different. It's the number times 2 each time. See—1 times 2, 2 times 2, 3 times 2, 4 times 2. . . .

Karen: That's the same, anyway.

Shoshana: It is not.

Karen: Yes, it is. If you add the same number, like 3 plus 3, it's just like multiplying that number by 2.

After the class was convinced of this by Karen, the teacher encouraged the students to go a step further.

Can any of you explain why your conjecture makes sense?

Joey: Yes. We thought that it goes up by 2 because you add one street and one avenue on each grid.

Sarah: We made a rule. The number of blocks is always the sum of the number of blocks on each side of the grid. See, that explains why. You have to go that many horizontally and that many vertically!

Can you make predictions about a really large grid, such as 50 by 50?

Lina Li: It would be a lot—maybe 200.

Kyle: I think it would be 100 or 150.

Karen: It's just like the little squares. It's one side plus the other side. So it's just 100.

Rectangles, Turns and Coordinates

What Happens

Session 1: Making Rectangles Students look at a transparency of the Teaching Resource, Which Are Rectangles?, and discuss the reasons why they think shapes are or are not rectangles. They discuss how to write a *Geo-Logo* procedure and draw rectangles. Following the whole-class segment, half the class works in pairs on the computers, writing procedures to draw three rectangles. The other half works on four Off-Computer Choices. Halfway through the work period, the groups switch.

Sessions 2 and 3: Rectangles, Coordinates, and Symmetry In Session 2, students use coordinates and the jumpto command to place their rectangles in different locations on the grid. They plan (off computer) and make (on computer) a symmetrical bulletin board. Half the class starts planning on the computer, and half starts planning off the computer. Halfway through the work period, the groups switch.

In Session 3, students finish their symmetrical bulletin boards on the computer. Off the computer, they work on other symmetry activities and any incomplete student sheets from Session 1. Halfway through the work period, the groups switch. At the end of the session, students discuss the work they did both on and off the computer.

Session 4: Properties of Rectangles Students analyze several *Geo-Logo* procedures to see if they draw rectangles. They use a general rectangle procedure that can draw any shape and size rectangle. Off computer, students plan how to draw and place three pictures on a grid using only the general rectangle procedure and the jumpto command.

Session 5: Turns Students finish working on grid pictures using the rect procedure. During the work period, half the students continue planning pictures off computer and half continue entering pictures on computer. Halfway through the work period, the groups switch. Students also analyze *Geo-Logo* rectangle procedures during their off-computer time. In a whole-class activity, students estimate the size of turns when turning their bodies, drawing paths on paper, and creating *Geo-Logo* commands to turn rectangles. They use a Turtle Turner (protractor) to estimate and measure turtle turns.

Sessions 6 and 7: Turning and Repeating Rectangles Students predict what will happen if a turn command is entered before a rect procedure. They learn to use the repeat command to rotate rectangles around the origin and to make multiple copies of rectangles. During the On-Computer Activity, they explore what happens when they write procedures using the repeat command and turns. Off computer, students complete the Assessment: Am I a Rectangle?

Sessions 8 and 9: Designing Rectangle Patterns Students make complex designs, drawing them first on Procedure Planning Paper, then entering them on the computer in the Rectangle Pictures activity. They create designs of their own using any of the commands they used in this unit.

Mathematical Emphasis

- Applying knowledge of coordinates to locate points on a computer screen

- Describing geometric figures such as rectangles and squares in several ways

- Understanding how *Geo-Logo* commands and patterns of commands reflect the properties of geometric figures

- Creating and applying patterns and mental arithmetic strategies to solve turtle geometry problems

- Using mirror and rotational symmetry to place rectangles on a grid and to design complex patterns of rectangles

What to Plan Ahead of Time

Materials

- Computers (Sessions 1–9)

- Apply Macintosh disk, *Geo-Logo* (Sessions 1–9)

- Computer disks for students to save their work

- Rulers, yardsticks, metersticks, or string: 1 per pair (Session 1)

- Scissors: 1 per pair (Sessions 3–4)

- Overhead projector (Sessions 1, 4–7)

- Printer (Sessions 2–3, 6–7, and 8–9, optional)

Other Preparation

- Duplicate student sheets and teaching resources (located at the end of this unit) as follows. If you have Student Activity Booklets, copy only the transparencies marked with an asterisk.

For Session 1

Which Are Rectangles?* (p. 168): 1 overhead transparency

Student Sheet 13, Procedure Planning Paper (p. 147): 3 per student

Student Sheet 14, Finding Rectangles in the Room (p. 150): 1 per student

Student Sheet 15, Finding Rectangles in the Drawing (p. 151): 1 per student

Student Sheet 16, Finding Rectangles on the Grid (p. 152): 1 per student

Student Sheet 17, Finding the Fourth Coordinate of Rectangles (p. 153): 1 per student

Student Sheet 18, What Is a Rectangle? (p. 154): 1 per student (homework)

For Sessions 2–3

Student Sheet 13, Procedure Planning Paper (p. 147): 1 per student

Student Sheet 19, Folding Lines (p. 155): 1 per student

Student Sheet 20, Drawing Symmetrical Patterns (p. 156): 1 per student

Student Sheet 21, Symmetry in the World (p. 158): 1 per student (homework)

Student Sheet 22, Drawing More Symmetrical Patterns (p. 159): 1 per student (homework)

Continued on next page

For Session 4

Student Sheet 13, Procedure Planning Paper (p. 147): 1 per student

Student Sheet 23, Planning Grid Pictures (p. 161): 1 per student

For Session 5

Student Sheet 24, Analyzing Rectangle Procedures (p. 162): 1 per student

360 Degrees* (p. 169): 1 overhead transparency

Turtle Turners* (p. 170): 1 overhead transparency

For Sessions 6–7

Turtle Turners* (p. 170) 1 transparency for every 4 students (cut each transparency into 4 Turtle Turners)

Student Sheet 25, Exploring Turns and Repeats with Rectangles (p. 163): 1 per pair

Student Sheet 26, Am I a Rectangle? (p. 164): 1 per student

For Sessions 8–9

Student Sheet 13, Procedure Planning Paper (p. 147): 2–3 per student

Student Sheet 27, Drawing Rectangle Patterns (p. 166): 1 per student

Student Sheet 28, Grids on Real Maps (p. 167): 1 per student (homework)

■ Work through the following sections of the *Geo-Logo* Teacher Tutorial:

Bulletin Board	109
Rectangle Pictures	112

■ Plan how to manage the computer activities.

If you have five to eight computers, have students work in pairs, and follow the investigation structure as written.

If you are using a computer laboratory, the lab is used in Sessions 1 to 8. You may wish students to do less extensive planning and checking off the computer, allowing them to refine their initial plans while working with *Geo-Logo* and using the additional Off-Computer Choices only when necessary.

If you have fewer than five computers, have students cycle through the computer activities as described in Managing the Computer Activities in This Unit, p. I-19. For Sessions 1, 2, 4, 6, 7, and 8, start students cycling through the computer immediately after introducing the On-Computer Activity, then work with the rest of the class to introduce the Off-Computer Choices. Make and post a schedule to use during the investigation, assigning about 20 minutes for pairs of students to use the computer(s) throughout the day. Students may have to complete their computer work for this unit as you begin a new unit or engage the rest of the class in a short session.

Making Rectangles

What Happens

Students look at a transparency of the Teaching Resource, Which Are Rectangles?, and discuss the reasons why they think shapes are or are not rectangles. They discuss how to write a *Geo-Logo* procedure and draw rectangles. Following the whole-class segment, half the class works in pairs on the computers, writing procedures to draw three rectangles. The other half works on four Off-Computer Choices. Halfway through the work period, the groups switch. Their work focuses on:

- Discussing students' definitions of rectangles.
- Identifying properties of rectangles—that they have four 90° angles and opposite sides that are equal in length.
- Using *Geo-Logo* commands to write procedures for drawing rectangles.

The chart on the next page shows how students work during this session.

Materials

- Rulers, yardsticks, metersticks, or string (1 per pair)
- Transparency of Which Are Rectangles?
- Student Sheet 13 (3 per student)
- Student Sheet 14 (1 per student)
- Student Sheet 15 (1 per student)
- Student Sheet 16 (1 per student)
- Student Sheet 17 (1 per student)
- Student Sheet 18 (1 per student, homework)
- Overhead projector
- Computers

Whole Class *20 min.*	**Identifying and Drawing Rectangles** **On-Computer Activity: Writing Rectangle Procedures** (Introduction) **Off-Computer Choices: Finding Rectangles** (Introduction)	
Two Groups (working in pairs) *20 min.*	Group A **On-Computer Activity** ■ Writing Rectangle Procedures	Group B **Off-Computer Choices** ■ Finding Rectangles in the Room ■ Finding Rectangles in the Drawing ■ Finding Rectangles on the Grid ■ Finding the Fourth Coordinate of Rectangles
Switch *20 min.*	**Off-Computer Choices** ■ Finding Rectangles in the Room ■ Finding Rectangles in the Drawing ■ Finding Rectangles on the Grid ■ Finding the Fourth Coordinate of Rectangles	**On-Computer Activity** ■ Writing Rectangle Procedures

Activity

Identifying and Drawing Rectangles

Introduce the session by having students tell everything they know about rectangles. Lead a discussion in which students suggest such ideas as: opposite sides equal, four equal angles produced by 90° turns, and opposite sides are parallel or "going in the same direction."

Show students a transparency of Which Are Rectangles? Ask students to share their reasons for why shapes are or are not rectangles. See the **Teacher Note**, Learning and Teaching Concepts (p. 50).

On the board or on a chart, list questions about which there is disagreement, such as these:

- Can a rectangle be slanted?
- Are squares rectangles?
- Do two opposite sides of a rectangle have to be longer than the other two opposite sides?
- Can a rectangle have rounded corners?

Tell students they are going to be drawing and defining rectangles throughout this investigation. They will continue to discuss the questions they have raised about rectangles. At this point, students should copy the questions about rectangles on Student Sheet 18 so they can research some additional answers for homework.

If you wanted to draw a rectangle using *Geo-Logo* commands, how might you do it?

Gather students around the computer display. Open the Bulletin Board activity in *Geo-Logo*. Using students' suggestions, type commands to draw a rectangle on the computer, such as the following:

fd 70

rt 90

fd 50

rt 90

fd 70

rt 90

fd 50

rt 90

Use the **Teach tool** to save the procedure for a demonstration in Session 2.

Note: It's best if the rectangle procedure you save for future demonstrations uses rt 90 (rather than lt 90) commands so it appears in Quadrant I. If students write a procedure that uses lt 90, ask them to write an additional procedure that uses rt 90; then save both procedures.

While you are entering the students' commands, review or demonstrate how to:

- enter the commands to draw a rectangle. Tell the class to make sure the turtle ends up facing, or heading, the same way it was when it started.
- click the **Teach tool** to define the procedure.
- test the procedure by entering the procedure's name in the Command Center.
- click the **Erase All tool.**
- save the work.

On-Computer Activity: Writing Rectangle Procedures

Introduce the on-computer Bulletin Board activity.

Tell students to open the Bulletin Board activity in *Geo-Logo* and write procedures to make at least three rectangles of different shapes and sizes. At least one of the rectangles should be a square. The last command for each procedure should turn the turtle so it is in the same direction as when it started.

Have students use the **Teach tool** to define each of their procedures. Tell them to save their work when they are finished.

Students will be using their computer rectangles tomorrow to make on-computer miniature bulletin boards. Therefore, they should copy at least one of their rectangle procedures onto Procedure Planning Paper (Student Sheet 13) in the right column under Commands.

Off-Computer Choices: Finding Rectangles

Ask students to look around the room and find things, such as window panes and books, that are rectangles. Show them how to make a right-angle tester or to use a corner of a piece of paper to check whether corners are 90°. While students are not working on the computer, they have a choice of working in pairs on Student Sheet 14, 15, 16, or 17. Introduce each of these choices by going over the instructions on the Student Sheet. Student Sheet 14, Finding Rectangles in the Room, asks students to move around the room in search of rectangles. Student Sheet 15, Finding Rectangles in the Drawing, gives students beginning experience with rectangles in perspective. Student Sheet 16, Finding Rectangles on the Grid, focuses on the connection between coordinates and rectangles. Student Sheet 17, Finding the Fourth Coordinate of Rectangles, goes more deeply into this connection. Students will need several copies of Student Sheet 13, Procedure Planning Paper, to complete Student Sheets 16 and 17. Note the special challenges on Student Sheet 17; these are rectangles that are not parallel to the axes, so the fourth coordinate is harder to find.

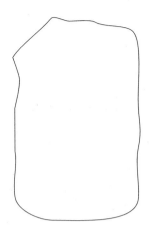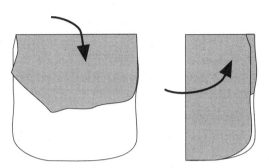

To make a right-angle tester, fold a piece of paper one way, then the other. This creates a reliable 90° angle.

Classroom Management

Assign students to work with partners at their seats on the Off-Computer Choices or at a computer on the On-Computer Activity. Remind students of the assignments and to save their work. Switch groups halfway through the work time.

Session 1 Follow-Up

 **Homework**

What Is a Rectangle?   Students work on answering the rectangle questions you listed on the board at the beginning of the session. They research the definition for rectangles in dictionaries or other books they may have at home, or they ask people outside of school how they would define a rectangle. Student Sheet 18 has a place to record the questions and the definitions they find.

❖ **Tip for the Linguistically Diverse Classroom**   Encourage students to interview people in their native languages.

Contrary to many people's belief, people frequently do not use definitions of concepts when they think; rather, they use "concept images." A concept image is a combination of all the mental pictures and properties we have associated with a concept. It also is strongly influenced by everything we have learned.

For example, students may see figures only in certain "standard" positions. They think that a turned square (◇) is no longer a square but is, instead, a diamond. They identify this figure (◁) as containing a right angle, but believe that this figure (△) contains a "left angle."

Even if they learn standard verbal descriptions or definitions of a concept, these limited concept images tend to rule their thinking. Therefore, students need to construct a meaningful synthesis of their verbal description with a wide variety of visual examples of the concept.

That is the reason the activities in this unit present many different examples of the concept *rectangle*. Further, they match nonexamples with examples to focus attention on critical attributes. For example, several different-size rectangles, rotated to different headings, should be seen alongside parallelograms, diamonds (actually, rhombuses), and other nonrectangles.

It is also important to help students construct a meaningful verbal synthesis from these examples. You are instrumental in encouraging them to become aware of both relevant characteristics (for a square: closed, four equal-length straight sides, four 90° angles) and irrelevant characteristics (size, orientation) and to synthesize the resulting rich visual images with a verbal definition—which we prefer to be the students' own.

What should you do if students claim, for example, that a rectangle has only two right angles? One approach is to ask for other opinions, without evaluating any of them. Then ask students to defend their opinions. A student might say that two of the angles are right angles but two are "left angles." In that case, you might have students try to convince one another that they are right. You could also ask clarification questions, such as, "If you turned the rectangle around, would the 'left angles' become right angles?" Or whether both "left" and right angles could be produced by having the turtle turn 90° (turning either left 90 or right 90, depending on which way it "went around the rectangle"). The goal is to have students think about their concepts and express and defend their thinking.

Rectangles, Coordinates, and Symmetry

What Happens

In Session 2, students use coordinates and the jumpto command to place their rectangles in different locations on the grid. They plan (off computer) and make (on computer) a symmetrical bulletin board. Half the class starts planning on the computer, and half starts planning off the computer. Halfway through the work period, the groups switch.

In Session 3, students finish their symmetrical bulletin boards on the computer. Off computer, they work on other symmetry activities and any incomplete student sheets from Session 1. Halfway through the work period, the groups switch. At the end of the session, students discuss the work they did both on and off the computer. Their work focuses on:

- Planning a project that involves exact measurement, description of rectangles, and specification of locations
- Using *Geo-Logo* to give coordinates for specific locations on the computer screen
- Placing rectangles symmetrically on a coordinate grid
- Finding folding lines in geometric shapes

The charts on the next page show how students work during these sessions.

Materials

- Student Sheet 13 (1 per pair)
- Student Sheet 19 (1 per pair)
- Student Sheet 20 (1 per pair)
- Student Sheet 21 (1 per student, homework)
- Student Sheet 22 (1 per student, homework)
- Scissors (1 per pair)
- Computers
- Printer (optional)

Session 2		
Whole Class *20 min.*	**Placing Rectangles on a Grid** **On-Computer Activity: Symmetrical Bulletin Boards** (Introduction) **Off-Computer Choices: Planning Symmetrical Bulletin Boards** (Introduction)	
Two Groups (working in pairs) *20 min.*	Group A **On-Computer Activity** ■ Symmetrical Bulletin Boards	Group B **Off-Computer Choices** ■ Planning Bulletin Boards ■ Folding Lines ■ Drawing Symmetrical Patterns
Switch *20 min.*	**Off-Computer Choices** ■ Planning Bulletin Boards ■ Folding Lines ■ Drawing Symmetrical Patterns	**On-Computer Activity** ■ Symmetrical Bulletin Boards
Teacher Check-point	**Making Symmetrical Bulletin Boards**	

Session 3		
Two Groups (working in pairs) *25 min.*	Group A **On-Computer Activity** ■ Symmetrical Bulletin Boards	Group B **Off-Computer Choices** ■ Folding Lines ■ Drawing Symmetrical Patterns
Switch *25 min.*	**Off-Computer Choices** ■ Folding Lines ■ Drawing Symmetrical Patterns	**On-Computer Activity** ■ Symmetrical Bulletin Boards
Teacher Check-point	**Making Symmetrical Bulletin Boards**	
Whole Class *10 min.*	**Discussing Symmetrical Patterns**	

Placing Rectangles on a Grid

Students share what they did for their homework assignment and what they found out about rectangles. Discuss whether any of the questions on yesterday's list can be answered and eliminated from the research questions.

Introduce the activity by opening *Geo-Logo* and the Bulletin Board activity on a computer with a large display.

Using **Open My Work** from the **File** menu, open the procedure that contains the rectangle you saved in Session 1.

Type the name of your saved rectangle procedure in the Command Center and press the **<return>** key.

Suppose I turned on the grid using the Grid tool. Where would the rectangle be?

Turn on the grid to show the students where it is. (If you used rt to draw your rectangle, it will appear in the lower-left corner of Quadrant I. If you used lt, it will be in Quadrant II.)

Use the **Erase All tool** to clear the drawing and the commands in the Command Center.

Suppose I wanted to place my rectangle somewhere else on the grid? How could I do that?

If someone suggests using the jumpto command, follow the student's suggestion, typing the jumpto command and its inputs on one line and the name of the rectangle procedure on the following line. If students do not suggest the jumpto command, introduce it as a possibility.

Use jumpto to move the rectangle to various locations, such as [50 –10] [30 40], and [–40 10]. Before pressing the **<return>** key, ask students to predict where the command will move the rectangle.

Ask students to make suggestions about how they could place the rectangle in other quadrants.

What commands could I write to place the rectangle entirely in Quadrant III?

Try several of the students' suggestions. It may take several attempts to find a command that will place the entire rectangle in Quadrant III.

On-Computer Activity: Symmetrical Bulletin Boards

In this investigation, we will be making a number of patterns with mirror symmetry. Such patterns have one or more lines on which they can be folded so that the two halves match one another. Some things that have symmetry are butterflies; hearts; guitars; and some letters. These things have matching halves, which means that a picture of each of these things can be folded on one or more lines so both halves cover each other exactly (see the **Teacher Note**, Pattern and Symmetry, p. 57).

On the computer today, we will try to make a symmetrical bulletin board. A symmetrical bulletin board has a rectangle in the same place in each of the four quadrants.

Open *Geo-Logo* and choose the Bulletin Board activity. Use the **Erase All tool** to clear the screen and the commands in the Command Center. Show students how to use the **Grid tool** to turn the grid on and off. Remind students how to use the jumpto commands: jumpto [20 40]. . . .

On the computer, place the rectangle you saved from Session 1 at a point in Quadrant I, using the jumpto command. Copy the computer drawing onto a piece of Procedure Planning Paper (Student Sheet 13) and hold up the paper for all to see.

This shows the rectangle in Quadrant I.

One way I can find where it would be in a symmetrical position in Quadrant II is to fold the paper along the vertical axis [*fold the paper along the vertical axis, with the drawing on the outside*] **and punch holes at the corners of the rectangle using something sharp** [*use a pen or pencil point to punch through both layers of paper*].

Open up the paper, showing the students the holes.

What commands could I now write to draw the rectangle in Quadrant II?

Try students' suggestions and see if they work.

Follow a similar procedure for placing a rectangle in Quadrant III by folding the paper horizontally and punching holes through the corners of the rectangle using something sharp. Then discuss the commands that would be necessary to draw the rectangle in Quadrant III.

You are to make a symmetrical bulletin board that has the same rectangle in each quadrant so that, if the paper is folded either horizontally or vertically, the rectangles will match. Half of you will use the rectangle procedure you recorded yesterday to plan your drawing before going to

the computer. The other half can start working on the computer and see if you can figure out where to place your rectangles. You and your partner should record the drawings and commands you enter on the computer on the Procedure Planning Paper because you may not finish your bulletin board this session. When you are finished with your symmetrical bulletin board, use the **Teach** tool and give the entire procedure a new name. Then save your work.

If you finish your first symmetrical bulletin board, you may wish to make another one using a different rectangle.

If a printer is available, you may want to have students print copies of their bulletin boards.

Note: If you have color monitors, show students how to add color to the bulletin boards with the setc command. This should be the last step in making the bulletin boards (see p. 121 in the *Geo-Logo* Teacher Tutorial).

(see p. 121 in the *Geo-Logo* Teacher Tutorial)

Activity

Off-Computer Choices: Planning Symmetrical Bulletin Boards

Explain to students that when they are not working on the computer, they are to plan their symmetrical bulletin boards.

When students are finished planning their bulletin boards, they can work in pairs on Student Sheet 19, Folding Lines, or Student Sheet 20, Drawing Symmetrical Patterns. Pass out copies of these sheets to each pair and briefly introduce them by going over the instructions.

Classroom Management

Some students may want to plan symmetrical bulletin boards on paper first, while other students may prefer to experiment on the computer, placing their rectangles in the four quadrants. You may want to respect this preference in work style when assigning students to work at the computer or on the Off-Computer Choices.

Students who are working at their seats should plan a procedure for placing one of their rectangles symmetrically in all four quadrants. If they finish their plan, they should finish their work on the student sheets from Session 1, then do Student Sheets 19 and 20.

Halfway through the work period, switch groups.

Teacher Checkpoint

Making Symmetrical Bulletin Boards

As students plan and input their symmetrical bulletin boards on paper and/or on the computer, observe how they work on the problem.

- Do students understand the problem? Do they fold their planning paper, or are they able to analyze where to place the figures in the different quadrants?

- How are students approaching the problem on paper and/or at the computer? Do they have a systematic way of looking at the problem? For example, do they plan the four points for one quadrant before determining them for another?

- Are students able to use what they have learned about coordinates? Do they guess randomly, or do they figure out the coordinates? Do they see the relationships among the coordinates in all four quadrants?

- Are students able to make and carry out a plan? Are the bulletin boards they create symmetrical? Are students able to see and explain why they are or are not symmetrical?

Discussing Symmetrical Patterns

During the last 10 minutes of Session 3, discuss the work students have been doing. Ask them to share some of their strategies for placing rectangles on the symmetrical bulletin boards. Ask them to share what they found out when they identified folding lines on Student Sheet 19, then share some of the symmetrical patterns they formed on Student Sheet 20.

Sessions 2 and 3 Follow-Up

 **Homework**

Symmetry in the World After Session 2, students look for examples of symmetry in the world. They bring in pictures to post on a symmetry bulletin board on the classroom wall, or they draw a picture of something around their home that has symmetry on Student Sheet 21.

Drawing More Symmetrical Patterns After Session 3, students continue their work drawing symmetrical shapes on a grid using Student Sheet 22.

Pattern and Symmetry

A pattern creates a regularity that can be copied. When we speak of patterns in fabric, we may mean a design made from colors or from textures. A plaid, for example, has a color pattern, and corduroy has a texture pattern.

All the designs illustrated below have patterns that allow you to know what piece is next. Take a moment and figure out what shape belongs where the question marks are in the illustrations.

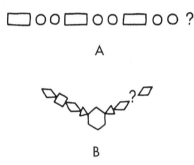

A

B

Patterns in which one-half can be flipped or folded over and land exactly on the other half, such as B, C, and E, have *mirror*, or reflective, symmetry. The two halves are *reflections* of each other. Design A, for example, will have mirror symmetry if the question mark is replaced with a rectangle, but not if it is replaced with a circle.

C

Patterns that revolve around a central point, such as D and E, have *rotational*, or circular, symmetry. A pattern with rotational symmetry can be turned a fraction of a circle—120° if it has three segments (as in D); 90° if it has four; 60° if it has six (as in E); 30° if it has twelve—and appear as if it hadn't moved at all. A circle has infinite rotational symmetry; any turn will leave it looking the same.

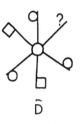

D

E

Some patterns with rotational symmetry—such as a circle, a regular hexagon like the yellow pattern block, any even-sided regular polygon, or E above—also have mirror symmetry. Others, such as the pinwheel D above, do not.

Session 4

Properties of Rectangles

Materials

- Student Sheet 13 (1 per student, and 1 transparency—optional)
- Student Sheet 23 (several per student)
- Computers
- Overhead projector (optional)

What Happens

Students analyze several *Geo-Logo* procedures to see if they draw rectangles. They use a general rectangle procedure that can draw any shape and size rectangle. Off computer, students plan how to place three pictures on a grid using only the general rectangle procedure and the jumpto command. Their work focuses on:

- Comparing *Geo-Logo* procedures for rectangles to examine similarities and differences in turtle descriptions of rectangles
- Describing how *Geo-Logo* commands and patterns of commands reflect the geometric properties of rectangles
- Discussing and using a rectangle procedure with variables to draw any shape and size rectangle
- Using the rect procedure and the jumpto command to draw and place pictures on a coordinate grid
- Using *Geo-Logo* measurement tools to decide if figures are or are not rectangles

The chart on the next page shows how students work during this session.

Session 4		
Whole Class *20 min.*	**Analyzing Rectangles** **Introducing the** rect **Procedure** **On-Computer Activity and Off-Computer Activity: Planning and Drawing Grid Pictures Using the** rect **Procedure** (Introduction)	
Two Groups (working in pairs) *20 min.*	Group A **On-Computer Activity** ■ Drawing Grid Pictures Using the rect Procedure	Group B **Off-Computer Choices** ■ Planning Grid Pictures Using the rect Procedure ■ Analyzing Rectangle Procedures
Switch *20 min.*	**Off-Computer Choices** ■ Planning Grid Pictures Using the rect Procedure ■ Analyzing Rectangle Procedures	**On-Computer Activity** ■ Drawing Grid Pictures Using the rect Procedure

 Ten-Minute Math: Lengths and Perimeters Two or three times during the next few sessions, have students do the activity Lengths and Perimeters outside of math time. Try the variation that involves the perimeters of regular polygons.

If necessary, you can introduce your students to the idea of perimeter by having them draw shapes on paper and walk around them with their fingers or by you creating masking tape shapes on the floor and having students walk around them.

Provide a perimeter problem such as the following:

The turtle was given the command repeat 4 [fd __ rt 90]. **When it was finished, the turtle had drawn a closed shape with a perimeter of 88 turtle steps. What shape did it make? What was the number for the** fd **command?**

Using Decimals Introduce the use of .5 into the problems. For example:

The turtle was given the command repeat 4 [fd 2.5 rt 90]. **How many steps did the turtle take?**

The turtle was given this command: repeat 4 [fd __ rt 90]. When it was finished, the turtle had drawn a closed shape with a perimeter of 42. What shape did it make? What was the number for the fd command?

Have students work in pairs for two or three minutes, sketching what they think the turtle drew and marking the lengths of the sides and the perimeter on their sketches.

Ask students to contribute their ideas. Students can demonstrate by acting out the turtle commands themselves.

For complete directions and variations, see p. 87.

Activity

Analyzing Rectangles

Ask for volunteers to write on the board or a chart a *Geo-Logo* rectangle procedure from their bulletin board work so the class can look for patterns in the procedures. To encourage students to see that the components of rectangles relate to the corresponding commands of the *Geo-Logo* procedures, ask them questions such as these:

What are some things that appear in every rectangle procedure?

What commands change in different rectangle procedures?

Students compare their rectangle procedures, listing the similarities (for example, the pattern of commands, that is, the order of the fd and rt commands; 90° input to the rotation commands) and differences (the input to the forward or back commands).

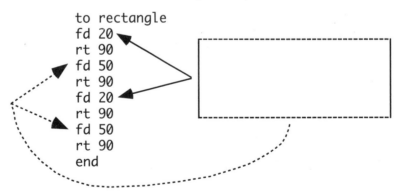

Introducing the rect Procedure

Introduce the idea of a general rectangle procedure.

Our *Geo-Logo* program has a procedure that you can use to draw rectangles of any size. The procedure uses only two numbers. What do you think these two numbers might be for? (One is for the length of one pair of opposite sides, the other is for the length of the other pair of opposite sides.)

Demonstrating the rect Procedure Using a large computer display, open the Rectangle Pictures activity and examine the rect procedure. Discuss the fact that the rect procedure contains the commands fd and rt and uses the variables L1 and L2 for side lengths. Type rect in the Command Center and press **<return>**.

What message did *Geo-Logo* send us? (rect needs more inputs) **What does it mean?** (The rect procedure must be given two numbers as inputs.)

Ask students for two numbers you can use with the rect command. Type rect followed by those numbers to draw a rectangle with those dimensions—for example, rect 20 60. Press the **<return>** key and discuss what happens.

Use the **Erase All tool** to clear the screen.

If I type rect 90 35 into the computer, what would the drawing look like?

Ask students to imagine the *Geo-Logo* rectangle in their minds. Then type rect 90 35 but do not press **<return>**. Students picture in their minds then draw what they think the turtle will draw. Then press **<return>** and ask students to compare their drawings with what they see on the screen.

For the next few days, we will be working with the rect procedure. We will be doing activities that involve using this procedure, along with the jumpto command, to create designs and pictures.

Note: If your class has experience with *Geo-Logo*, you may wish to have them write their own rect procedure instead of showing them the already written procedure.

On-Computer Activity and Off-Computer Activity: Planning and Drawing Grid Pictures Using the rect Procedure

Your task is to draw one or more of the these pictures [*show students the pictures on Student Sheet 23, Planning Grid Pictures*].

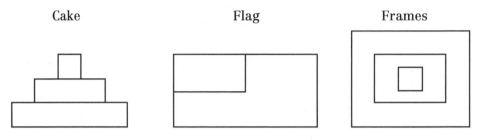

Cake   Flag   Frames

You can use only two types of commands:

■ the jumpto **command to place the turtle so it can draw each rectangle**

■ the rect **procedure to do the drawing**

Give each student a copy of Student Sheets 13 and 23. Tell students they will plan their *Geo-Logo* procedures on the Procedure Planning Paper (Student Sheet 13). Then go over the instructions for drawing the pictures on Student Sheet 23.

Remind students they are to use only the jumpto and rect commands. Review what each command does and what the numbers used with each mean. Remind them they will need to click the **Grid tool** to see the grid when they work on the computers.

Option If your students need additional guidance, work with the whole class to create one design, such as the cake. Have the class suggest how to draw the cake (on a transparency of the Procedure Planning Paper, Student Sheet 13) and write a *Geo-Logo* procedure (such as the procedure at the right).

Highlight the mathematics they are using, including geometry and mental arithmetic. At the computer, emphasize correcting mistakes instead of "erasing and starting over." This is called "debugging."

```
to cake

jumpto [0 0]

rect 20 100

jumpto [20 20]

rect 20 60

jumpto [40 40]

rect 20 20

end
```

Classroom Management

Students will have two sessions to plan the Grid Pictures and enter them on the computer. They begin the activity during this session (Session 4) and finish it during Session 5.

Some students will plan their pictures on Procedure Planning Paper (Student Sheet 13) before entering them on the computer. Other students will begin their work on the computer, then have more time later to do more planning on paper. Divide the class into two groups, one of which starts working in pairs on the computer, the other of which starts off the computer.

Students who begin working at the computer should record their commands on Procedure Planning Paper and save their work so they can finish their plans off the computer. Remind them to use the **Grid tool** so they can work on a grid.

Students who begin working at their seats should plan their Grid Pictures on Procedure Planning Paper. They can choose the order in which to do the pictures and the size and the exact location for each picture. Halfway through the work period, switch groups, as shown on the chart.

While Students Are Working This is an excellent time to observe students' mathematical thinking. The **Teacher Note**, Working on Rectangle Pictures (p. 65), discusses the work of a girl who understood basic geometry and measurement but did not analyze relationships of figures and had difficulty with negative coordinates.

Note: If you have color monitors, show students how to add color to the pictures with the `setc` command. Remind them that this should be the last step in making the pictures (see p. 121 in the *Geo-Logo* Teacher Tutorial).

Session 4 Follow-Up

Extensions

Using Computer Tools to Analyze Rectangles You may wish to show students how to use the **Label Length tool** and the **Label Turn tool** to "double-check" that the rectangles they drew on the computer have opposite sides that are the same length and that all turns are 90° (see *Geo-Logo* Teacher Tutorial, p. 124).

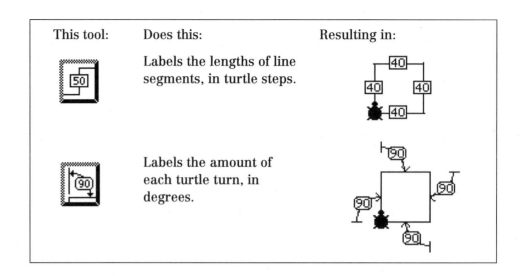

This tool:	Does this:	Resulting in:
	Labels the lengths of line segments, in turtle steps.	
	Labels the amount of each turtle turn, in degrees.	

That's a "Piece of Cake" For students who might be interested, suggest they try to make the cake *sideways*. Ask if *that* is a "piece of cake."

Working on Rectangle Pictures

Teresa wants to draw a picture of three concentric rectangles. The teacher started the class by giving three commands:

```
jumpto [0 0]
rect 50 100
jumpto [10 10]
```

Teresa draws the picture on her Procedure Planning Paper. To find the length and width of the second inner rectangle, she counts the number of "blocks" in the picture. She does not use the lengths of the outer rectangle or the coordinates of the corners to find length and width (she did not even use the coordinates for a rectangle with the lower-left corner at [0, 0]).

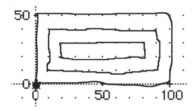

She writes: rect 30 80.

Next, Teresa knows she has to make the turtle jump to the lower-left corner of the next rectangle, the smallest one.

She writes jumpto [10 10] and looks at her teacher for approval. She erases it and asks, "Is it (10, 20)?"

The teacher replies, "What do you think?," which prompts her to say, "It is (20, 10)" and write that in her sequence of instructions.

Counting again, Teresa decides on the last command rect 10 60. Her final procedure before going to the computer is this:

```
jumpto [0 0]
rect 50 100
jumpto [10 10]
rect 30 80
jumpto [20 10]
rect 10 60
```

Teresa enters her procedure at the computer and complains that the turtle does not jump to the right place. She says, "I want the turtle here," pointing to (20, 20).

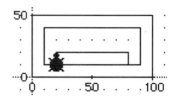

The teacher asks her what the coordinates of that point are. She does not know and begins guessing but finally changes jumpto [20 10] to jumpto [20 20].

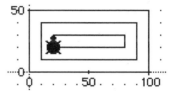

The teacher asks Teresa to draw the same picture beginning at the point (–100, 50). She begins planning her procedure:

```
rect 50 100
jumpto [10 10]
rect 30 80
```

She does not write a jumpto command to move the turtle to the (–100, 50) and seems to think of the coordinates of the inner rectangle only as they relate to the outer rectangle.

She says, "They're the same commands as before."

The teacher asks her to type these commands. It is not until then that she notices the picture is not where the teacher requested.

The teacher asks, "What's wrong?"

Continued on next page

Teresa knows the turtle must begin at (–100, 50) but does not know how to name these coordinates. The teacher reminds her of the streets and avenues metaphor, and Teresa finds the coordinates with some effort.

She has difficulty finding the second set of coordinates and is even more frustrated trying to find the third pair. She finally realizes that the inputs to the jumpto commands follow a pattern. She uses her pattern to find the coordinates for the last jumpto command. This was the first time anyone observed Teresa creating her own pattern in mathematics.

The teacher wrote notes summarizing that Teresa appeared to have a good understanding of distances, lengths, the fd and rt commands, and how the commands related to the geometry of a rectangle. She did not yet, however, analyze the figure and determine how the measures of different rectangles within the same design were related to one another (other students, for example, would have figured out that the inner rectangles must have side lengths 20 less than the next larger one).

Further, Teresa understood how to find coordinates, but only in a limited sense. She had great difficulty with negative coordinates, which was compounded by her lack of skill in counting by tens in a negative direction.

As her next project, Teresa wanted to draw a three-layer cake. The commands that drew her cake follow:

```
jumpto [-50 0]
rect 30 50
jumpto [-40 30]
rect 20 30
jumpto [-30 50]
rect 10 10
```

This time Teresa did not have any problem finding the coordinates for jumpto. She marked them off with a big dot, and although she was still counting to figure out the inputs of jumpto, she was doing it correctly.

The teacher observed that Teresa did not count to find the inputs of the first rect command. She knew the first input was 50 since the rectangle began at –50 and ended at 0. The teacher asked her "How do you know it is 50?"

Teresa said, "Because it goes from negative 50 to 0."

The teacher observed that to figure out the length of the next rectangle she did not count but used the relationship the first rectangle (the bottom) had with the next layer.

The teacher asked her "How did you find this 30?"

Teresa said, "You take 20 off 50," pointing to the bigger rectangle and then to the empty ends left by the next.

She was so successful with this project that she added a little candle at the top of her cake, with some help from the teacher.

Turns

What Happens

Students finish working on grid pictures using the `rect` procedure. During the work period, half the students continue planning pictures off computer and half continue entering pictures on computer. Halfway through the work period, the groups switch. Students also analyze *Geo-Logo* rectangle procedures during their off-computer time. In a whole-class activity, students estimate the size of turns when turning their bodies, drawing paths on paper, and creating *Geo-Logo* commands to turn rectangles. They use a Turtle Turner (protractor) to estimate and measure turtle turns. Their work focuses on:

- understanding turns as a change in orientation or heading
- exploring what happens when turns are repeated—such as discovering that four 90° turns leave you facing the same direction as when you started
- becoming familiar with degrees as a common measurement for turns
- understanding there are 360° in one full turn, 180° in a half turn, and 90° in a quarter turn
- estimating turn measures for 30°, 45°, 60°, 90°, 120°, and so on

The chart on the next page shows how students work during this session.

Materials

- Student Sheet 24 (1 per student)
- Transparency of 360 Degrees
- Transparency of Turtle Turners
- Choice Time materials from Session 4
- Overhead projector
- Computers

Whole Class 10 min.	Off-Computer Activity: Analyzing Rectangle Procedures (Introduction)	
Two Groups (working in pairs) 15 min.	**Group A** **On-Computer Activity** ■ Drawing Grid Pictures Using the `rect` Procedure (finish)	**Group B** **Off-Computer Choices** ■ Planning Grid Pictures Using the `rect` Procedure (finish) ■ Analyzing Rectangle Procedures
Switch 15 min.	**Off-Computer Choices** ■ Planning Grid Pictures Using the `rect` Procedure (finish) ■ Analyzing Rectangle Procedures	**On-Computer Activity** ■ Drawing Grid Pictures Using the `rect` Procedure (finish)
Whole Class 20 min.	**Turning Your Body**	

Activity

Off-Computer Activity: Analyzing Rectangle Procedures

Introduce Student Sheet 24, Analyzing Rectangle Procedures, by discussing the first example, which is already done on the sheet.

Look at the commands in the example. Why did the person working the problem make the changes? Are there any other ways to change the commands so they draw a rectangle?

Turning Your Body

Note: This activity is a repeat of an activity in the grade 3 unit, *Turtle Paths*, with the addition of 45° turns. If your students are familiar with turns, you may want to do just a quick review. The **Teacher Note**, Turns and Angles (p. 72), discusses some important points about Turtle Turners.

What is a turn?

Students may suggest that a turn is a change in direction or heading.

Suppose a robot was facing the front of the room and I wanted it to turn and face the back of the room. What commands could I write?

Students might state rt 90 followed by another rt 90 (or lt 90 lt 90). A couple of students might suggest rt 180. If students are having difficulty understanding the idea, you might demonstrate.

I begin facing the front and make a lt 90 and another lt 90 [*turn and pause between turns*]. I am now facing the back of the room. But what if I make a fast, nonstop turn [*demonstrate*]? Can I write that with one command?

Have students stand at their seats, facing the front of the room, and figure out the answers to the following questions by turning their bodies. Ask students to share their reasoning.

Do a rt 90 and another rt 90. What is one more command that will have us face the front of the room again?

How many rt 90 turns do I have to make to turn all the way around?

I make three lt 90 turns. How can I write that in one command?

(Accept both lt 270 and rt 90. Have students discuss why they end up in the same position.)

Ask students to visualize and point to where they would be after 1, 2, 3, or 4 rt 90 or lt 90 turns. Then have them perform the turns to check. Here, and in the following activities, occasionally have students close their eyes when they turn.

Show the 360 Degrees transparency. Tell students that the turtle makes 360 very small turns to turn all the way around. The amount of each turn is called a degree—a right turn 90 is a turn of 90 degrees.

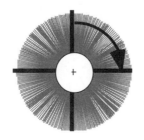

Turns Less than 90° Introduce turns that are smaller than right turns by stating the following:

What if I wanted to make a turn that was smaller than a 90° turn? For example, how much would I turn if I wanted to face the corner of the room instead of the windows?

Accept students' suggestions. Most should agree that the turn will be a number smaller than 90°.

How much should I turn if I wanted to make a turn that is exactly half a 90° turn?

Ask students to try it, and accept students' ideas about the measure of the turn. Establish that the measure is 45°, half of 90°.

Ask students to stand again and pretend there is a huge clock on the floor with the 12 at the front of the room and the 6 at the back. Have students be the hands in the center of the clock. With them facing the front of the room, both arms extended to the front (12:00), they rotate one arm to a 3:00 position, then turn their bodies (keeping arms stationary) to show a rt 90.

Ask students to again face front with their arms extended at 12:00, move one arm to 1:00, and then turn their bodies to face one o'clock.

If I wanted to write a turtle command to turn this much, what should I write?

Accept ideas from students, asking them to state their reasons. It may be helpful for students to turn their bodies through several hours of the clock, identifying appropriate turtle commands for larger angles before figuring out the command for moving from 12:00 to 1:00.

> "If I turn from 12:00 to 6:00, the command is rt 180."

> "If I turn from 6:00 to 4:00, the command is lt 60."

Introduce the Turtle Turner Show a Turtle Turner on the overhead. Students describe it, paying particular attention to the direction the turtle is facing, the distinction between lt and rt, and the symmetry between the left and right-hand sides. Demonstrate how to use the Turtle Turner to draw angles. Place the Turtle Turner so that the center of the turtle is at the end of the line and the double arrow lies along the line the turtle drew. From this placement, students can read out various turns. Ask students to show on the overhead the angle through which the turtle turns to illustrate 30°, 45°, 90°, 120°, and other turns.

Tell students they will be using turns in Sessions 6, 7, 8, and 9 to tilt rectangles and design rectangle patterns.

Note: In this unit, we emphasize turns that are multiples of 30° and 45°— 30°, 45°, 60°, 90°, 120°, 135°, and so on.

If there is time, play on the overhead a game where you (and later a student) point to a line and challenge someone to come up and point to the line that is 60° to the right of your line, 120° to the left of your line, and so on. Emphasize the use of the 90° turns as reference measures (for example, "It was partway between 90° and 180°, but closer to 90°, so I estimated 120°"). Check the accuracy of the estimates by using the Turtle Turner to measure the turn.

Classroom Management

Students continue the On-Computer Activity and Off-Computer Choices they started in Session 4.

If necessary, review the properties of all rectangles and of the rect procedure and how these two are connected.

Can any rectangle you can think of be drawn by the rect procedure? (Remember that you could turn the turtle before giving the rect command.)

Is everything the rect procedure draws a rectangle? Why or why not?

Divide the class into two groups. Assign one group to work in pairs on the computers and the other group to work on the Off-Computer Choices. Students working at the computers should finish their grid pictures. Students working off the computer should first finish planning or fixing their grid pictures, then finish Student Sheet 24, Analyzing Rectangle Procedures. Halfway through the work session, switch the groups.

Teacher Note ⟩ *Turns and Angles*

Understanding angles and angle measures is critical to understanding geometric shapes such as triangles and squares. Turtle turning is a powerful and dynamic way to learn about these concepts. In order to take advantage of the potential of turtle turning, students must understand just how turtle turns relate to the shapes the turtle draws.

When students are using Turtle Turners, they need to understand the relationship between the angle that the turtle turns and the angle that is formed when the turtle moves forward in its new direction. For example, the following picture shows the turtle's position after starting on the left, then moving forward 100 toward the right.

fd 100

The next picture shows the position of the turtle and the new direction it is facing after it turns left 120°.

lt 120

Below are the results of the turtle moving forward 100 in the new direction.

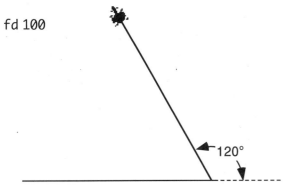

fd 100

Note that when the turtle moves forward after turning, the angle that it draws is a 60° angle. Even though the turtle has turned through 120°, the lines it draws form a 60° angle.

In Grades 3 and 4, we are concerned mainly with the measure of the angle the turtle has turned (120°), not with the measure of the angle

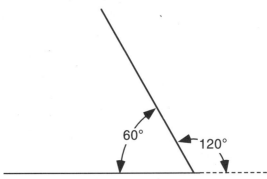

that is drawn (60°), but in later grades students will work with both. It is important for students to note this difference at the beginning of their work with Turtle Turners.

Notice that with 90° turns, the amount the turtle turns and the measure of the drawn angle are the same:

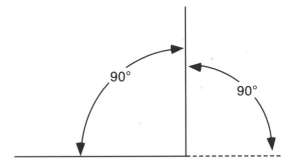

To ensure students are developing sound concepts, you might find it useful to continually check they are visualizing and representing the correct angle through which the turtle turns (120° in the first set of pictures above). When discussing turns with students, it helps to ask them to sweep out the turn with their hands and turn their bodies.

Even though we are not concerned with the measure of the angle the turtle draws in turtle turning, students might come to see that the more the turtle turns, the *smaller* the angle produced by drawing the next line will be.

A final historical note: The Egyptians and Babylonians may have divided the circle into 360 equal parts because the year was believed to have 360 days: one degree for one day of the sun's path around the earth.

Turning and Repeating Rectangles

What Happens

Students predict what will happen if a turn command is entered before a
`rect` procedure. They learn to use the `repeat` command to rotate rectangles around the origin and to make multiple copies of rectangles. During the On-Computer Activity, they explore what happens when they write procedures using the `repeat` command and turns. Off computer, students complete the Assessment: Am I a Rectangle? Their work focuses on:

- using turn commands to turn and rotate a rectangle
- using the `repeat` command to explore multiple turns
- using knowledge of the properties of rectangles to identify rectangles and nonrectangles
- writing *Geo-Logo* procedures using the `rect` command (and, in some instances, turn commands), for pictured rectangles

The chart below shows how students work during these sessions.

Materials

- Student Sheet 25 (1 per pair)
- Student Sheet 26 (1 per student)
- Turtle Turners (1 per student)
- Computers
- Printer (optional)

Sessions 6 and 7		
Whole Class *40 min.*	**Turning Rectangles** **Repeating Rectangles** **On-Computer Activity: Exploring Turns and the** `repeat` **Command** (Introduction) **Off-Computer Activity: Assessment: Am I a Rectangle?** (Introduction)	
Two Groups (pairs on computer; individuals off computer) *40 min.*	Group A **On-Computer Activity** ■ Exploring Turns and the `repeat` Command	Group B **Off-Computer Activity** ■ Assessment: Am I a Rectangle?
Switch *40 min.*	**Off-Computer Activity** ■ Assessment: Am I a Rectangle?	**On-Computer Activity** ■ Exploring Turns and the `repeat` Command

Turning Rectangles

Open *Geo-Logo* and the Rectangle Pictures activity, using the large display (if one is available).

Today I'm going to use some turn commands with the rectangles we've drawn on the computer. See if you can predict what will happen.

Use **Open My Work** to open the rectangle procedure you wrote in the first session of this Investigation. Use your demonstration rectangle procedure to draw a rectangle.

First I'll make a rectangle with the rect **command. Give me two numbers for inputs.**

I'm now going to type rt 90 *before* **the** rect **command. What do you think will happen to the drawing on the screen?**

Use the **Erase All tool** to clear the Command Center and Drawing window. Type the two commands on one line, without pressing the **<return>** key—for example, rt 90 rect 40 60.

Accept several predictions about what will happen from students. Then press the **<return>** key to show them what happens.

Ask students if the picture on the screen is still a rectangle. If there is disagreement, have students review their definitions of rectangles to help them decide.

Delete the turn command and rerun the rect command to place the rectangle back in the original position.

Let students predict what will happen if you use other turn amounts, such as rt 45, lt 30, rt 120, rt 180, and lt 150, followed by a rect command. After each set of predictions, show students what happens on the screen.

Note: In general, you do not have to type commands one to a line; you can type them one after another, with a space between them. Pressing the **<return>** key directs the turtle to execute an entire line of commands. It is important to put the turn command and the rect command on the same line, so students can predict what will happen before they see the turtle turning. See the **Teacher Note**, What's a Rectangle? What's Not? (p. 77).

There is a *Geo-Logo* command we can use if we want to repeat a group of commands. It's called the `repeat` command, and this is how it works.

Suppose I write the procedure `rt 90 rect 60 40`. What will the turtle draw?

Type the command, but don't press the **<return>** key. Have students share their ideas. Demonstrate what happens on the computer by pressing the **<return>** key.

Type the same commands again on the next line, so the screen looks like this:

```
rt 90 rect 60 40
rt 90 rect 60 40
```

Now there are two commands that are the same. What do you think will happen when I press the <return> key?

If students are not sure, you may want to add a third line with the same commands.

Next, use the **Erase All tool,** then ask:

What do you think will happen if I typed this command `repeat 2 [rt 90 rect 60 40]`? Notice that I have to put brackets around the command.

Ask students to predict what will happen before you press the **<return>** key.

How would I change the command to repeat a rectangle 3 times? 4 times? What would happen if I changed the `repeat` number to 5?

After students' predictions, try the examples on the demonstration computer.

What happened when we tried `repeat 5`? Why?

Explain the instructions for Student Sheet 25, Exploring Turns and Repeats with Rectangles. Students are to use the student sheet while they are working at the computer in the Rectangle Pictures activity. Tell students this activity will give them an opportunity to see what happens as they vary commands using `fd`, `bk`, and `repeat`.

Off-Computer Activity: Assessment

Am I a Rectangle?

Students work individually on the problems on Student Sheet 26, Am I a Rectangle? Emphasize that thinking about the properties of rectangles and about reasons and justifications is more important than finishing all the problems on the sheet. Suggest that students use their Turtle Turners to test whether angles are right angles and to determine how many degrees a rectangle has been turned. Remind students that the rect procedure needs two inputs and that turning the turtle first is allowed and sometimes is necessary.

Collect students' Am I a Rectangle? (Student Sheet 26) sheets and assess their solutions and justifications.

- Do they correctly categorize rectangles and nonrectangles?
- Are their explanations based on visual, descriptive, or analytic ideas?
- Do they link the properties of a rectangle to the rectangle procedure? See the **Teacher Note**, Writing About Rectangles (p. 78).

❖ **Tip for the Linguistically Diverse Classroom** Have limited English proficient students convey how they know figures are not rectangles by circling key parts (for example, where lines do not connect, where a figure curves, or where angles are not 90°).

Classroom Management

Divide the class into two groups. Assign one group to work in pairs on the computer, using Student Sheet 25, Exploring Turns and Repeats with Rectangles. Assign the other group to work individually to complete Student Sheet 26, Am I a Rectangle? Students can begin one activity in Session 6 and continue the same activity in Session 7. Partway through Session 7, switch groups.

Sessions 6 and 7 Follow-Up

 **Extension**

Computer Rectangles Challenge To extend the discussion about rectangles, show other shapes similar to those on Student Sheet 26, Am I a Rectangle?, on the computer screen. See How to Use Rectangles Challenge in the *Geo-Logo* Teacher Tutorial (p. 118).

What's a Rectangle? What's Not?

After successfully drawing the tilted rectangle (Student Sheet 26) with the rect procedure

( ) by first turning the turtle, students often say that the parallelogram ( ) can also be drawn with the rect procedure. They are surprised when it does not work, and many reflect on the difficulty, finally concluding that the non-rectangular parallelogram cannot be drawn because it does not have 90° turns. For example, two girls who were working on the parallelogram had the following discussion.

Marci: I don't think that you can do it. [*She was then ready to go on to next problem.*]

Luisa: Yes, you can.

Marci: You can't because—

Luisa: Let's try it.

The students try it on the computer and observe the result.

Marci: You can't do it because the turns are not 90.

Marci did not feel it was necessary to try this example; she actually had a good reason for her belief, but, in the face of conflict, decided not to share it. She seemed to need to have her idea validated on the computer before she was willing to argue it publicly.

Another student had a similar experience. In response to the parallelogram, Emilio said, "Maybe it could be drawn with the rectangle procedure." He estimated the initial turn, then the side lengths. After typing his commands, he

got a rectangle. He held the sheet up right next to the screen, and said, "No."

Could you use different inputs, or is it just impossible?

Emilio: Maybe if you used different inputs. [*He types the initial turn. He stares at the picture of the parallelogram. Pauses.*] No, you can't [*pauses*]. Because the lines are slanted, instead of a rectangle going like that [*traces*].

Yes, but this one's slanted [*indicates the tilted rectangle Emilio had successfully drawn*].

Emilio: Yeah, but the lines are slanted. This one [*the rectangle*] is still in the shape of a rectangle. This one [*the parallelogram*], the thing's slanted. This thing [*the rectangle*] isn't slanted. It looks slanted, but if you put it back it wouldn't be slanted. Anyway you move this [*the parallelogram*], it wouldn't be a rectangle. [*Shakes his head.*] So, there's no way.

Emilio didn't even complete his second attempt. Rather, after making the initial turn and trying to decide on the inputs, he recognized that the relationship between adjacent sides was not consistent with the *Geo-Logo* definition. The first attempt with *Geo-Logo* and "running through the procedure in his head" contributed to his emerging sense of certainty.

Similarly, some students may not even try making the square with their rectangle procedure, saying "It's a square, not a rectangle."

The teacher was examining responses to Student Sheet 26, Am I a Rectangle? What might she conclude?

First, she believes Teresa has a working knowledge of what are rectangles and what are not rectangles. Teresa also grasped such geometric ideas as "closed shape."

What should we say about her use of the term slanted? We shouldn't "mark her down" for not using technical terms. Teresa seemed to understand the difference between rectangles that are slanted (5) and figures that are not rectangles (6).

Teresa remains, however, at a visual level of knowledge. Figures "look like" or "don't look like" rectangles to her. She could answer questions about properties, but she uses a visual way of thinking when she writes her justifications.

When the teacher asked her about slantedness, Teresa replied, "In figure 5, the whole figure is slanted, but in figure 6, the sides are slanted." She expressed important ideas, which would be more powerful if elaborated. For Teresa and many other fourth graders, class discussions of the idea of "slantedness" can usually be beneficial.

Designing Rectangle Patterns

What Happens

Students make complex patterns, drawing them first on Procedure Planning Paper, then entering them on the computer in the Rectangle Pictures activity. They design patterns of their own using any of the commands they used in this unit. Their work focuses on:

■ Analyzing *Geo-Logo* procedures and drawings

■ Predicting drawings from commands and commands from drawings

■ Designing rectangle patterns using *Geo-Logo*

The following charts show how students work during these sessions.

Materials

■ Student Sheet 13 (2–3 per student)

■ Student Sheet 27 (1 per student)

■ Student Sheet 28 (1 per student, homework)

■ Computers

■ Printer (optional)

Session 8		
Whole Class *20 min.*	**On-Computer Activity: *Geo-Logo* Rectangle Patterns** (Introduction) **Off-Computer Activity: Drawing Rectangle Patterns** (Introduction)	
Two Groups (working in pairs) *20 min.*	Group A **On-Computer Activity** ■ *Geo-Logo* Rectangle Patterns	Group B **Off-Computer Activity** ■ Drawing Rectangle Patterns
Switch *20 min.*	**Off-Computer Activity** ■ Drawing Rectangle Patterns	**On-Computer Activity** ■ *Geo-Logo* Rectangle Patterns
Teacher Check-point	**Designing *Geo-Logo* Rectangle Patterns**	

Session 9		
Two Groups (working in pairs) *20 min.*	**Group A** **On-Computer Activity** ■ *Geo-Logo* Rectangle Patterns	**Group B** **Off-Computer Activity** ■ Drawing Rectangle Patterns
Switch *20 min.*	**Off-Computer Activity** ■ Drawing Rectangle Patterns	**On-Computer Activity** ■ *Geo-Logo* Rectangle Patterns
Teacher Check-point	**Designing *Geo-Logo* Rectangle Patterns**	
Whole Class *20 min.*	**Discussing *Geo-Logo* Rectangle Patterns**	

On-Computer Activity: *Geo-Logo* Rectangle Patterns

We can use the `rect` procedure to create and analyze some interesting and complex computer designs.

Using the large display, open *Geo-Logo* and the Rectangle Pictures activity. Close the Drawing window by choosing **Hide Drawing** from the **Windows** menu so students won't see what the turtle is drawing.

Type the following commands (if you do not have a large display, you may want to write them on a transparency or on the board):

```
rect 100 10
rect 90 20
rect 80 30
```

This is the beginning of a computer pattern that uses only rectangles. Look at the commands. Predict what the next command will be.

Students should give a reason for their prediction. After students have had an opportunity to respond, type the next command: `rect 70 40`.

What do you think this pattern looks like? Take a couple of minutes and make a sketch of what the turtle will draw.

After all students have made sketches, ask for volunteers to share their sketches with the class. Have them draw the sketches on the board and share their reasoning for their drawings.

Open the Drawing window by choosing **Show Drawing** from the **Windows** menu.

Does the drawing match your predictions?

How did the turtle make the drawing—what did the turtle draw first, second, and so on? How do you know?

Teach the computer your procedure and run the procedure. (Teaching and then running the procedure will cause the turtle to draw the procedure more slowly, so students have time to observe the order in which the turtle draws the rectangles.)

Have students help you edit the procedure in the Teach window. Ask them what the next command should be. Rerun the procedure to see the edited drawing.

Tell students they will have an opportunity to complete this pattern and make other patterns during these last two sessions. (Don't finish the pattern in the computer demonstration.)

Distribute Student Sheet 27, Drawing Rectangle Patterns, and a copy of Student Sheet 13, Procedure Planning Paper. Tell students that both procedures on Student Sheet 27 will produce interesting patterns. Have them choose one procedure, copy it onto Procedure Planning Paper, and sketch it before trying it on the computer.

Off-Computer Activity: Drawing Rectangle Patterns

Classroom Management

All students will need to draw the patterns from Student Sheet 27 on Procedure Planning Paper (Student Sheet 13) before trying them on the computer. Therefore, if there are any students who did not finish exploring turns and the `repeat` command on the computer, you may wish to have them work on the computers first while other students are drawing patterns.

As pairs of students finish drawing one of the patterns on paper, assign them to work on the computer. After they have drawn one of the patterns on the computer, allow them to design a pattern of their own. Depending on the classroom flow at this point, students may be able to design their pattern on the computer. If many students are sharing a few computers, students should do much of the work on their own designs off-computer, on Procedure Planning Paper.

When students have designed patterns they like and drawn them on the computer, they can teach them and save them on the computer. If a printer is available, students can print their drawings and the commands for them. Have students save their work on a floppy disk so they can show the rest of the class their procedure on the large display at the end of Session 9.

Activity

Teacher Checkpoint

Designing *Geo-Logo* Rectangle Patterns

Observe students as they create their rectangle patterns. Students will vary in how they approach this problem.

Many students will investigate patterns on the computer, trying out various commands to see what happens. They may edit the commands after seeing the results or just go on and try something new.

Other students will plan their patterns on paper first. They may draw a pattern on paper, then try to find commands to draw the pattern on the computer. Or they may write a series of commands on paper, execute the commands on paper to see the pattern they formed, then try the commands on the computer.

Geo-Logo provides an environment in which both planning and exploration lead to new insights. As students work, ask them to explain what they are doing:

- Do they have a plan?
- Are they exploring to see what happens?

Also observe the following:

- Are students able to predict what will happen before they run a command?
- Are they able to explain what happened and why after the turtle runs a command?

In this activity, the work students do in designing a pattern is more important than the final patterns they create. It is also important that they be able to describe the connections between their commands and their drawings.

Activity

Discussing *Geo-Logo* Rectangle Patterns

At the end of Session 9, have students discuss and share the patterns they designed. Ask for volunteers to open the work they saved on a disk and show it on the display computer.

Have them describe the process they went through to create their pattern.

Students may want to show only the commands first and ask the class for predictions about the patterns. Or they may want to show the drawings and ask the class how they might have written the commands. Or they may want to present both the commands and the drawings together. Provide time for a question-and-answer period after each student's presentation.

Choosing Student Work to Save

As the unit ends, select one of the following options for creating a record of students' work on this unit.

- Students look back through their folders or notebooks and write about what they learned in this unit, what they remember most, and what was hard or easy for them. You might have students do this work during their writing time.

- Students select one or two pieces of their work as their best, and you also choose one or two pieces of their work to be saved. This work is saved in a portfolio for a year. You might include students' written solutions to the assessment, Am I a Rectangle? (Investigation 2, Session 6), and any other assessment tasks from this unit. Students can create a separate page with brief comments describing each piece of work.

- You may want to send a selection of work home for families to see. Students write cover letters, describing their work in this unit. This work should be returned if you are keeping a year-long portfolio of mathematcis work for each student.

Sessions 8 and 9 Follow-Up

Grids on Real Maps Many maps are printed with a grid for purposes of measurement and location (for example, lines of longitude and latitude) or location only (for example, rows and columns identified by numbers and letters). Have students collect and examine a number of such maps and explain the purpose of the grid for each. If students do not have maps at home, they should draw a map of a room in their house on Student Sheet 28. They should add a grid, place furniture on the grid, then make a "key" to show the location of each piece of furniture.

Geo-Logo Project Students learn more effectively if they are encouraged to explore the computer and *Geo-Logo*'s turtle geometry in open-ended situations. Ask students to plan and enter the commands for a picture— another bulletin board or any other type of picture—using any commands and shapes they wish. They can do this using the Rectangle Pictures activity. For examples, see the **Teacher Note**, Example Projects (p. 85). If you have regular access to computers, you might have students work on their own projects during free periods throughout the year.

Longitude and Latitude   Students may wish to investigate and report on the coordinate system—longitude and latitude—used by those at sea.

Checkers by Mail   Using coordinates, students may play a game of checkers, Grid Tic-Tac-Toe, or Sunken Ships with students from another building, state, or country, by mail.

Example Projects

Vanessa drew a cake as her project. She wrote her rectangle procedures without any problems, counting the spaces to determine the lengths and widths.

She next tried `jumpto [0 10]` then `jumpto [0 50]`, saying, "I've always had a little problem with that." She carefully counted by tens and figured out that she needed a `jumpto [10 50]`.

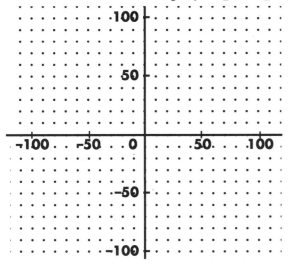

At this point Vanessa switched the **Grid tool** on, saying "Now it's going to be hard." She had planned `jumpto [10 70]`, but seeing where the turtle ended up, she changed the input to [10 80] then to [20 80]. As a result of seeing her drawing on the screen, she changed her idea of what she wanted.

Vanessa typed her candle procedure. She then looked at her figure and decided that she did not like the way her candles were spread apart on the paper and decided not to do it as she had it in her drawing.

She counted on from [20 80] and entered `jumpto [40 80]` and then `candle`.

The teacher asked her if she could figure out the next `jumpto` from her commands without counting. She said that it would be `jumpto [80 80]`, probably adding 40 to her previous `jumpto`. But when she saw it, she changed the input to [70 80] then to [60 80]. She typed a final `jumpto [80 80]` and `candle` which completed the first cake.

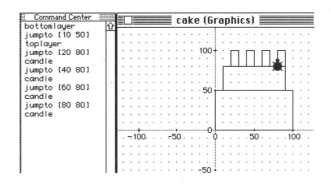

Vanessa wasn't satisfied with the location of her candles and wanted to move two over. She moved directly to the correct `jumptos`, changing them to [10 80] and [30 80]. Her confidence indicated that she understood the connection between each command and its effect.

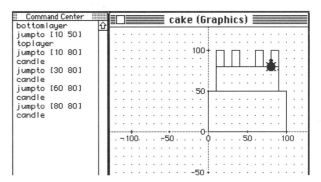

The teacher learned a lot observing Vanessa at work.

- Because Vanessa counted spaces to determine lengths, she understood these measures and how to determine them.

- She could estimate coordinates, so she had a "number sense" about them, but often did not use the grid to determine them exactly.

- Because she counted from one coordinate to another, she understood how coordinates related to each other. Other students, wanting to move the turtle from (10, 20) to (15, 30), incorrectly enter the difference: `jumpto [5 10]`.

- Overall, Vanessa had the ability to plan a solution.

Continued on next page

■ She approached the mathematical problems systematically, though she still preferred trial-and-error to planning in advance. However, she did use the numbers she had already entered as a basis for her revision, so even her trial-and-error work was systematic and based on mathematical intuitions.

As further illustrations, here are projects from other students.

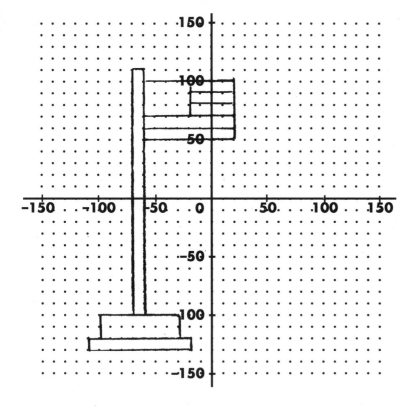

To Starsandstripes

Jumpto [-100 -120]
rect 20 70
Jumpto [-110 -130]
rect 10 90
Jumpto [-70 -100]
rect 210 10
Jumpto [-60 50]
rect 50 80
Jumpto [-60 70]
rect 30 40
Jumpto [-20 80]
rect 10 40
Jumpto [-60 60]
rect 10 80

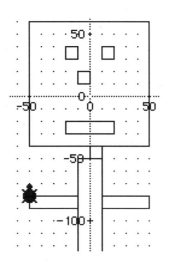

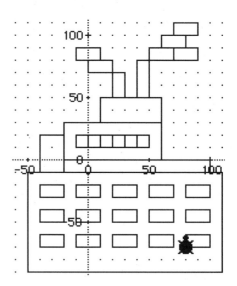

Lengths and Perimeters

Lengths and Perimeters is an off-computer problem using the *Geo-Logo* repeat command.

Basic Activity

Students try to visualize the results of a repeat command given to the *Geo-Logo* turtle. First they work with length. Given a total distance (for example, 72), they think of repeat commands that will send the turtle that distance (for example, repeat 6 [fd 12]). By working with these commands, they are working with factors and multiples.

Students also do this activity with shapes. Given a perimeter of a regular polygon, they figure out the repeat command to make that shape. Or given the repeat command, they figure out the perimeter. Other variations involve rectangles.

Students focus on:

- relating factors to their multiples
- recognizing, visualizing, and drawing polygons
- relating the perimeter of a polygon to the lengths of its sides
- using multiplication, division, addition, and subtraction in the context of the perimeters of polygons

Materials

- Calculators (optional)
- Computer with large demonstration screen and the *Geo-Logo* disk for *Sunken Ships and Grid Patterns* (optional)

Procedure

Note: The repeat command is not formally presented in this unit, although it is available for students to use on the computer. If your students have not used the repeat command, you will need to introduce it the first time you do this activity. For hints, see the Special Notes on the next page.

Step 1. Choose a distance that you want the turtle to go. For example, What could we do so the turtle would go 35 turtle steps?

Step 2. Students write down commands to move the turtle that distance. Working in pairs, students spend two or three minutes writing down all the *Geo-Logo* commands using repeat that they can think of that would send the turtle that distance. For example, for 35 turtle steps, these commands would work:

repeat 5 [fd 7]

repeat 7 [fd 5]

repeat 35 [fd 1]

repeat 1 [fd 35]

Students can use calculators to test their ideas.

Step 3. Make a list on the board or overhead of all the different responses. Ask students how they know that the commands work. Students can use skip counting, demonstrate with concrete materials, or explain their mental strategies to prove their answers. Ask if they have all the possibilities. How do they know? Could 3 work? What about 9? What about 14? How do they know?

Variations

Perimeters of Regular Polygons These problems either provide the perimeter of a shape and students have to find out the length of a side, or they give the length of a side and students have to determine the perimeter. Here are some examples:

- The turtle was given this command: repeat 4 [fd __ rt 90]. When it was finished, the turtle had drawn a closed shape with a perimeter of 40 turtle steps. What shape did it make? What was the number for the fd command?

Continued on next page

- The turtle made a regular hexagon—a six-sided shape just like the yellow pattern block. The perimeter of the hexagon was 72 turtle steps. Find the number for the blank in the command it used: repeat 6 [fd __ rt 60].

- The turtle made a triangle with this command: repeat 3 [fd 35 rt 120]. What is the perimeter of the triangle?

In these problems, encourage students to sketch what they think the turtle drew and to mark on their sketch the lengths of the sides and the perimeter. Ask students to act out what the turtle did by walking its path on the floor.

Perimeters of Other Shapes These problems involve shapes in which all the sides are not equal. Here are some examples:

- The turtle made a rectangle using the following command: repeat 2 [fd 20 rt 90 fd 10 rt 90]. What did the rectangle look like? What is its perimeter?

- The turtle made a rectangle with a perimeter of 50. It made the shape with this command: repeat 2 [fd 12 rt 90 fd __ rt 90]. What is the missing number in the fd command?

- The turtle made a rectangle with a perimeter of 50. It made the shape with this command: repeat 2 [fd __ rt 90 fd __ rt 90]. What are the missing numbers in the two fd commands? Is there more than one set of numbers that will work?

Make sure students sketch what they think the turtle drew and mark on their sketch the lengths of the sides and the perimeter. As you walk around the room, you can easily see from their sketches what students understand and what is confusing for them as they visualize the turtle's movements. You may also want to have students act out the turtle's movements.

Using Decimals Introduce the use of .5 into the problems. For example:

- The turtle was given the following command: repeat 4 [fd 6.5]. How many turtle steps did it take?

Discuss the meaning of .5 (for ways to develop this idea, see the grade 3 unit, *Mathematical Thinking at Grade 3)*. Students can try the problem mentally, then test their ideas on the calculator.

Special Notes

The repeat Command in *Geo-Logo* If your students have not yet used the repeat command on the computer, you will have to spend the first ten-minute math session introducing this command.

Write a repeat command on the board—for example, repeat 20 [fd 2]. Explain that the directions inside the bracket are done over and over again, as many times as the number following the word repeat. So repeat 20 [fd 2] means: take two turtle steps (that's the first time), take two turtle steps (that's the second time), take two turtle steps (that's the third time), continue taking two turtle steps until you've done that 20 times.

Have students act out a few different repeat commands. Be sure they try some examples that have more than one command in the brackets. For instance, repeat 4 [fd 40 rt 90] means that the turtle will do the two commands fd 40 rt 90 four times:

fd 40 rt 90 fd 40 rt 90 fd 40 rt 90 fd 40 rt 90

See the *Geo-Logo* Teacher Tutorial for more information on using the repeat command (p. 121).

Perimeter If students are not familiar with the word *perimeter*, explain that it is the distance around the outside of a closed shape. Draw a closed shape on the board and say:

If an ant started here and walked all the way around the shape until it came back to where it started, it would have walked around the shape's perimeter.

Put some closed shapes on the floor with tape and have students walk around their perimeters. Ask them how far they went. They can find solu-

Continued on next page

tions in paces or in standard measures (for related activities on linear measure, using non-standard and standard units, see the grade 3 unit, *From Paces to Feet*).

Testing Students' Commands on the Computer If a computer with a large demonstration screen is available, you can test students' commands so that all students can see the results. Otherwise, students can test the commands on their own later at the computer. Use the Free Explore activity in *Geo-Logo*.

There are several ways to test students' repeat commands to see if the turtle travels the correct distance.

■ First, have the turtle make the line (for example, fd 35). Then bring the turtle back to the beginning of the line and test each of the student's repeat commands to see if they bring the turtle the same distance.

■ Draw a line of the correct length (for example, 35 turtle steps). Position the turtle so that it will draw a line parallel to the first line. This lets students more easily compare their lengths.

■ Use the **Ruler tool** in *Geo-Logo* to measure the lines made by students' repeat commands. However, keep in mind that it is easy to be off by one or two turtle steps when measuring with the Ruler. When using the Ruler with decimals, you will want to make sure that numbers are displayed using one decimal point (change the number of decimal places by selecting **Decimal Places** from the **Options** menu).

The following activities will help ensure that this unit is comprehensible to students who are acquiring English as a second language. The suggested approach is based on *The Natural Approach: Language Acquisition in the Classroom* by Stephen D. Krashen and Tracy D. Terrell (Alemany Press, 1983). The intent is for second-language learners to acquire new vocabulary in an active, meaningful context.

Note that *acquiring* a word is different from *learning* a word. Depending on their level of proficiency, students may be able to comprehend a word upon hearing it during an investigation, without being able to say it. Other students may be able to use the word orally, but not read or write it. The goal is to help students naturally acquire targeted vocabulary at their present level of proficiency.

We suggest using these activities just before the related investigations. The activities can also be led by English-proficient students.

Investigations 1–2

mail carrier, post office, address, letters, deliver

1. On the board, draw and identify a *post office* and a block of houses with a *mailbox* in front of each.

2. Holding a stack of *addressed* and stamped *letters*, pretend you are a *mail carrier* making *deliveries* to the homes on the board.

   I deliver mail in this neighborhood. Let's see whom the first letter goes to. It's to the Cruz family at 3465 Oak Street.

ship, sink, sunk

1. On the board, draw and identify a *ship* on some waves.

2. Next draw a hole in the ship. Point to the ocean as you explain how water is starting to leak into the boat. Say that the ship will soon *sink*.

3. Now draw the same ship at the bottom of the ocean. Explain that the ship has *sunk*.

Teacher Tutorial

Contents

Overview

The units in *Investigations in Number, Data, and Space* ask teachers to think in new ways about mathematics and how students best learn math. Units such as *Sunken Ships and Grid Patterns* add another challenge for teachers—to think about how computers might support and enhance mathematical learning. Before you can think about how computers might support learning in your classroom, you need to know what the computer component is, how it works, and how it is designed to be used in the unit. This Tutorial is included to help you learn these things.

The Tutorial is written for you as an adult learner, as a mathematical explorer, as an educational researcher, as a curriculum designer, and finally —putting all these together—as a classroom teacher. Although it includes parallel (and in some cases the same) investigations as the unit, it is not intended as a walk-through of the student activities in the unit. Rather, it is meant to provide experience using the computer program *Geo-Logo* and to familiarize you with some of the mathematical thinking in the unit.

The first part of the Tutorial is organized in sessions parallel to the unit. Included in each session are detailed step-by-step instructions for how to use the computer and the *Geo-Logo* program, along with suggestions for exploring more deeply. Many sessions include suggested questions for reflecting on your mathematical thinking. The second part of the Tutorial includes more detail about each component of *Geo-Logo* and can be used for reference while working through the Tutorial or later during the unit. There is also detailed help available in the *Geo-Logo* program itself.

In *Sunken Ships and Grid Patterns*, students use *Geo-Logo*, a learning environment designed for mathematical, particularly geometric, exploration. Using *Geo-Logo*, students are able to construct paths and geometric shapes in addition to observing them. Since one of the best ways to learn something is to teach it, *Geo-Logo* uses the metaphor of "teaching the turtle" how to move, turn, and draw. Writing a list of instructions for how to construct a shape encourages students to think carefully about geometric properties and to use geometry-oriented language.

Geo-Logo is a rich learning environment intended to be used for open exploration. In the unit, students are introduced to the environment by playing a game and guiding a taxi through a grid of streets. The later activities are progressively more open, ending with "Free Explore." The Tutorial is organized in the same way, beginning with directed tasks intended to help you become familiar with the environment and commands and then opening up for you to explore more on your own. For this reason, it might be best to start at the beginning and work through the sessions in order. Teachers new to using computers and *Geo-Logo* can follow the detailed step-by-step instructions. Teachers with more experience might follow the main directions without needing to read all the step-by-step instructions.

As is true with learning any new approach or tool, you will make mistakes, be temporarily stumped, go down wrong paths, test out hypotheses, and so on. This is all part of learning but may be doubly frustrating because you are dealing with computers. It might be helpful to work through the Tutorial and the unit in parallel with another teacher. If you get particularly frustrated, ask for help from the school computer coordinator or another teacher more familiar with using computers. It is not necessary to complete all the sessions in the Tutorial before beginning to teach the unit. You can work through the sessions in parts as you prepare for parallel investigations in the unit.

Although the Tutorial will help prepare you for teaching the unit, you will learn most about *Geo-Logo* and how it supports the unit as you work side-by-side with your students.

Note to teachers: These directions assume *Geo-Logo* Ships & Grids has been installed on the hard disk of your computer. If not, see How to Install *Geo-Logo* on Your Computer, p. 130.

☞ 1. **Turn on** the **computer** following the usual procedure for your computer or by doing the following:

   a. If you are using an electrical power surge protector, switch to the **ON** position.

   b. Switch the **computer** (and the monitor, if separate) to the **ON** position.

   c. Wait until the desktop appears.

Your computer screen may look something like this:

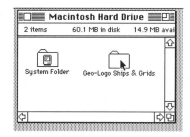

☞ 2. **Open** *Geo-Logo* by doing the following:

   a. **Double-click** on the *Geo-Logo* Ships & Grids folder icon if it is not already open. To double-click, click twice in rapid succession without moving the pointer.

   b. **Double-click** on the *Geo-Logo* Ships & Grids icon in this folder.

   c. **Wait** until the *Geo-Logo* opening screen appears. Single click anywhere on the window.

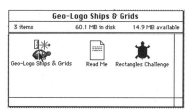

Depending on your computer, you may see other things on the screen in addition to or behind the *Geo-Logo* windows. These are other computer functions that may be available to you but are not part of *Geo-Logo*. If you click one of these by mistake, you can return to *Geo-Logo* by clicking into any *Geo-Logo* window or selecting *Geo-Logo* from the desktop. For additional information, see Trouble-Shooting, p. 126.

How to Start an Activity

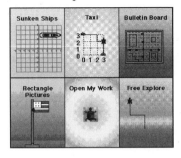

Start an **activity** or game by doing the following:

☞ 1. **Click** on the **[Sunken Ships]** square (or the square for any activity you wish).

When you choose an activity, the Tool window, Command Center, Drawing window, and Teach window for that activity fill the screen.

A dialogue box appears with directions for how to get started.

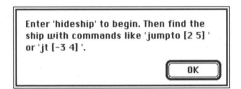

Enter 'hideship' to begin. Then find the ship with commands like 'jumpto [2 5]' or 'jt [-3 4]'.

OK

☞ 2. **Click** on **[OK]** or press the **<return>** key to close the dialogue box.

The Sunken Ships game is on the computer screen.

Should you need them, trouble-shooting notes are included on p. 126.

How to Play Sunken Ships

The turtle in *Geo-Logo* is a robot that follows your commands.

Throughout the Tutorial, you will command the turtle to turn and move along various paths and to jump to different locations. For Sunken Ships, you write `jumpto` commands to move a boat over grid intersections that may be above a sunken ship.

This is the story behind the Sunken Ships game: A long time ago, a pirate ship containing treasures sank to the bottom of the sea. You are part of a team of scientists on a boat searching for the sunken ship. The boat has a special tool that can tell if part of a ship is directly beneath it. Your job is to move the boat to grid locations on the surface of the ocean and beam down to see if you can find the sunken ship. The ship is under five intersection points on the grid. To find the ship, you must locate all five points.

☞ 1. Instruct the program to draw a grid above the sunken ship by doing the following:

    a. **Type** `hideship` in the Command Center. (The blinking vertical line, called the text cursor, shows where any typed text will go. It is currently in the Command Center.)

    b. **Press** the **<return>** key.

Hideship is a *Geo-Logo* group of commands, called a procedure, that contains the commands to draw a grid over a sunken ship. When you type hideship in the Command Center and press **<return>**, *Geo-Logo* carries out the procedure and draws the grid.

The hidden ship is under five intersection points along a straight horizontal or vertical line. The object is to find all five points using the fewest number of jumpto commands.

☞ 2. Tell the program where to jump to in order to look for the coordinate points of the sunken ship by doing the following:

        Type jumpto and two coordinate points between brackets, such as jumpto [3 4], on the line after hideship. **Press** the **<return>** key.

Notice that the *Geo-Logo* command jumpto uses square brackets and no comma between numbers for the coordinates of a point, instead of parentheses with a comma normally used for coordinates. In *Geo-Logo*, parentheses and commas have been reserved for a different meaning.

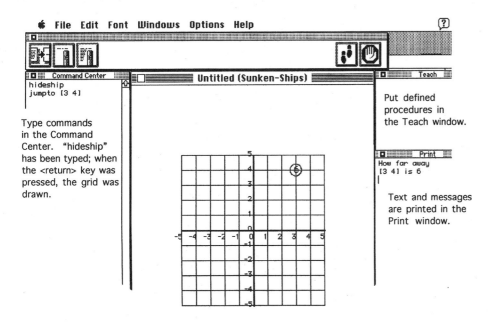

Try your own commands or follow these steps:

Suppose you want to go to the middle of the upper-left quadrant.

> **a. Type** jumpto [-3 4].
>
>   You can use the **<delete>** key to correct errors when typing commands.
>
> **b. Press <return>.**

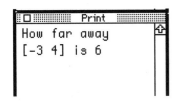

Notice the Print window at the lower right of the screen. Each time you jump to a location, in the Print window *Geo-Logo* indicates whether you found part of the ship. If you did, it reports the discovery of the ship, such as "[1 2] is the ship!". If you did not, it tells you how far away the point is from the nearest undiscovered point on the ship, such as [–3 4] is 6.

If the turtle does not understand a command, *Geo-Logo* writes a message in a dialogue box. For help with these messages, see the section *Geo-Logo* Messages, p. 128.

☞ **3.** Continue to **enter** jumpto **commands** until you find all five points of the sunken ship.

You might want to use the abbreviation jt for jumpto.

When you have found all five points, *Geo-Logo* draws the ship and tells you how many jumpto commands you used.

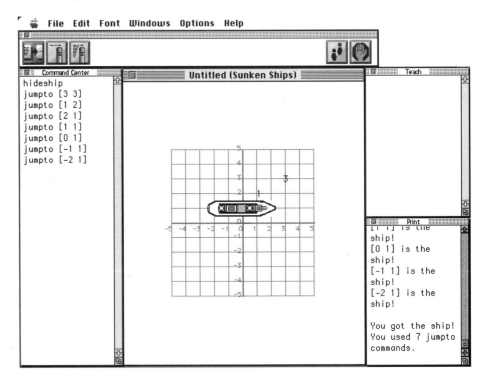

If you wish, keep a record of how many jumpto commands you used before playing another game of Sunken Ships.

Above the Command Center is a row of buttons labeled with pictures of tools that are available to use in this activity. For a description of each tool, see More About Sunken Ships, p. 100. To choose one of these tools, click on the button.

☞ 4. To play another game, **Click** the **Erase All tool** . That will clear the Command Center and Drawing window. As before, type hideship, press **<return>**, and enter jumpto commands to find all five points on the sunken ship.

☞ 5. **Pause and Reflect.** You might want to pause for a bit and reflect on your mathematical thinking in this activity. Here are some questions you might consider:

   ■ What strategy did you use for your first guess?

   ■ What strategy did you use for subsequent guesses?

   ■ How is the grid in Sunken Ships like or unlike other coordinate grids?

How to Finish an Activity

☞ 1. **To Finish a round** of Sunken Ships

   Click the **Erase All tool** .

   The computer is ready to start a new game of Sunken Ships. If others will be playing the game, you may want to leave the screen like this instead of quitting *Geo-Logo* and shutting down the computer.

   If you have finished working on Sunken Ships, you can close that activity and begin another activity by following step 2, or you can close *Geo-Logo* completely by following step 3.

☞ 2. **To Finish** working on the current **activity** (in this case, Sunken Ships):

   Choose **Close My Work** from the **File** menu.

   a. **Move the mouse pointer** over the word **File** in the menu title bar along the top of the screen.

   b. **Press** and **hold** the mouse **button** until the menu items appear.

   c. Continue to press the mouse button as you **drag** the **pointer** down and select **Close My Work**.

   d. **Release** the mouse **button**.

A dialogue box may appear asking whether you wish to save your work. If you want to save your work, see How to Save Your Work on p. 106. If not, click **Don't Save**.

You are ready to begin another activity.

☞ 3. **To Finish** using *Geo-Logo*:

Choose **Quit** from the **File** menu.

☞ 4. **To Finish** using the **computer**:

a. Follow the usual procedure to shut down your computer.

b. **Turn off** the **computer** (and monitor, if separate).

More About Sunken Ships

Special tools are available in each activity and displayed in the Tool window. Some are necessary for the activity, such as **Erase All** in Sunken Ships, and are explained in the instructions. Others might enrich the activity but are not necessary to complete it, such as **Step** in Sunken Ships.

The tool window for Sunken Ships:

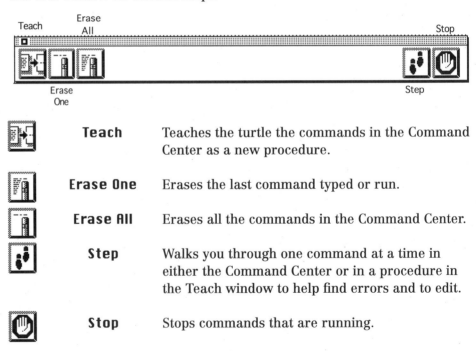

	Teach	Teaches the turtle the commands in the Command Center as a new procedure.
	Erase One	Erases the last command typed or run.
	Erase All	Erases all the commands in the Command Center.
	Step	Walks you through one command at a time in either the Command Center or in a procedure in the Teach window to help find errors and to edit.
	Stop	Stops commands that are running.

- For more details about these and other tools, see Tools on p. 124.

- To record your thoughts and observations about your work, choose **Show Notes** from the **Windows** menu. To close Notes, choose **Hide Notes** from the **Windows** menu or click the close box on the left of the Notes title bar.

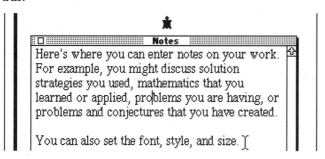

- You can enlarge all letters in the Command Center and Teach window for easier viewing. Select **All Large** from the **Font** menu. Select **All Small** to change back to normal.

How to Choose a New Activity

☞ 1. Choose **Change Activity** from the **File** menu.

A dialogue box may appear asking whether you wish to save your work. If you want to save your work, see How to Save Your Work on p. 106. If not, click **[Don't Save]**.

☞ 2. **Single-Click** on the new activity button on the *Geo-Logo* opening screen, in this case **[Taxi]**.

How to Use Taxi

Open *Geo-Logo* and select **[Taxi]**, following steps 1 and 2 in Getting Started with *Geo-Logo* on p. 95.

A dialogue box appears with instructions.

> Teach the turtle a short path that goes to every house, then back to the "H."
> Enter 'map' to begin.
>
> [OK]

Click **[OK]**.

In the Taxi activity, the turtle travels along streets and avenues to go to houses. To see the streets, avenues, and houses, follow these steps:

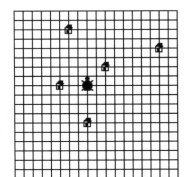

☞ 1. Type map and press **<return>**.

Map is a *Geo-Logo* procedure that contains the commands that draw a map and five houses. When you type map in the Command Center and press **<return>**, *Geo-Logo* carries out the map procedure and draws the map and houses.

The object of Taxi is to write commands to move the turtle along the streets and avenues to go to each of the five houses and back to the beginning using the least number of steps. The turtle robot knows commands to move and to turn, such as these:

fd 50	forward 50	moves the turtle forward 50 steps (or whatever number you want)
bk 10	back 10	moves the turtle back 10 steps (or whatever number you want)
rt 90	right turn 90 degrees	turns the turtle right 90 degrees (use only 90 for Taxi)
lt 90	left turn 90 degrees	turns the turtle left 90 degrees (use only 90 for Taxi)

In Taxi, each block on the map is ten turtle steps. All turns are 90 degrees. (Note, however, that the turtle will follow move or turn commands with any number.)

☛ 2. **Enter commands** in the Command Center to make the turtle go to a house. Try your own commands or follow these steps:

Suppose you want the taxi to go to the top left house first. Remember that each block on the map represents ten turtle steps:

a. **Type** fd 60 **and press <return>.**

You can use the **<delete>** key to make changes, if needed.

b. **Type** lt 90 **and press <return>.**

The turtle rotates 90° on its belly to make a left turn.

c. Continue to type commands to make the turtle go to the house.

When the turtle reaches a house, the picture of the house flashes and appears larger.

If the turtle does not understand a command, it will write a message in a dialogue box. For help with interpreting these messages, see the section *Geo-Logo* Messages, p. 128.

To edit or change your commands, press the **<delete>** key to move the cursor back over the incorrect text and erase it. Then type new text and press **<return>**.

You can also use the mouse to select words or blocks of text by dragging over the text (pressing and holding down the mouse button as you move the mouse). When the text is highlighted, press **<delete>** to erase it and type the new text.

Each time you change a command and press **<return>**, *Geo-Logo* redraws the path using the new command.

☛ 3. **Enter commands** and press **<return>** to make the turtle go to the other four houses. Remember that you can erase any commands you entered and start over with a new strategy.

Since the objective is to go to all five houses and return to the beginning using the least number of turtle steps, you may want to think through the paths first or draw them on paper before entering them on the computer. Or you may wish to try two or three different paths on the computer and compare the numbers of steps for each.

Above the Command Center are *Geo-Logo* tools you can use in this activity. With these tools you can erase the last command you entered or erase all the commands in the Command Center.

 Erase One erases the last command entered.

 Erase All erases everything in the Command Center.

In *Geo-Logo*, you can teach the turtle to remember a set of commands you entered, such as how to travel along a certain path to reach all five houses, as one procedure. Later, you can command the turtle to follow the procedure, to travel that path, by entering the name of the procedure in the Command Center.

Try teaching the turtle a procedure for Taxi by completing step 4.

 4. **Teach** the turtle your path by following these steps:

    a. **Click** the **Teach tool** .

       When you click the **Teach tool**, you define this list of commands as a procedure. The computer asks you to type a name for the procedure.

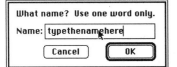

    b. **Type** a one-word name for the procedure (you can use letters and numbers) such as **taxi1**. (Note that since *map* has already been used to name a procedure, you cannot use it.)

    c. Press **<return>** or click **[OK]**.

The commands disappear from the Command Center and the procedure appears in the Teach window, defined by the name you gave it. Notice that the computer adds a first and last line to your commands. The first line says *to* **taxi1** (or the name you chose) and the last line says *end*. The procedure also includes the procedure map that draws the map.

Geo-Logo clears the Drawing window in preparation for your next entry.

You now have taught the turtle how to move along a path in a certain way. If you want the turtle to do this again, run your procedure following these steps:

 5. **To run** your procedure:

    a. **Enter** your **procedure** by typing its name (such as **taxi1**) in the Command Center. If necessary, move the text cursor (the blinking vertical line that shows where any typed text will go) into the Command Center by clicking the mouse in that area.

    b. **Press <return>**.

If you want to change your procedure, edit it in the Teach window. Click your cursor in that window, press the arrow keys to move up or down and use the **<delete>** key to erase text. Then type your changes.

☛ 6. **Click** the **Erase All tool** to erase everything in the Command Center and Drawing window in preparation for drawing a new path.

Notice that any procedures you defined are still available in the Teach window.

☛ 7. **Enter commands** to draw a different path to all five houses. You might try to find a shorter path or decide to go to houses in a different order. Teach the new procedure.

☛ 8. **Record** your procedures on Student Sheet 10, Taxi. Figure out the total length of each path in turtle steps.

Use the **Label Lengths tool** to help you find the total length of the path. Remember to account for any parts of the path you retraced.

☛ 9. **Print** your work, if possible.

   a. **Check** that your printer is connected and turned on.

   b. **Choose Print** from the **File** menu. If the Drawing window does not print completely, select "Color/Greyscale" in the Print dialogue box.

It is sometimes interesting to see a "hard copy" (a copy printed on paper) of your *Geo-Logo* work. Printing is not a required part of the *2-D Geometry: Sunken Ships and Grid Patterns* unit. However, you might want to include printing when you work with students, depending on the availability of a printer and your classroom setup.

☛ 10. Assistance with *Geo-Logo* windows, vocabulary (commands), tools, and directions, as well as hints, is available from the **Help** menu at any time.

   a. **Choose Windows** from the **Help** menu. When you have finished looking at this **Help** screen, click on the **[Done]** button.

   b. **Choose** each of the other **Help** titles—**Vocabulary**, **Tools**, **Directions**, and **Hints**—to see what is available.

☛ 11. **Pause and Reflect.** You might want to pause for a bit and reflect on your mathematical thinking in this activity. Here are some questions you might consider:

   ■ How did you decide which commands to use?

   ■ How did you know how many steps to move?

- When you wanted to turn, how did you know whether to use rt or lt?

- If you combined commands, what math thinking did you use?

- What strategy did you use to find the path with the least number of turtle steps?

- What did you do to find the total number of turtle steps in your path?

You have now completed Taxi. Before you finish using the computer or start another activity, save your work as explained below.

How to Save Your Work

When you turn off the computer or start a new activity, the computer memory is cleared of all commands and procedures to make room for new ones. To avoid losing your work, you can save it on a disk before the computer memory is cleared. Once your work has been saved on a disk, you can open it again to show it to someone or work on it some more.

To save your work, follow these steps:

 1. Choose **Save My Work** from the **File** menu.

    (⌘ S—To save using the keyboard, hold down the **<⌘>** key and press the **<S>** key.)

The first time you save your work, a dialogue box such as the following will appear asking for a name.

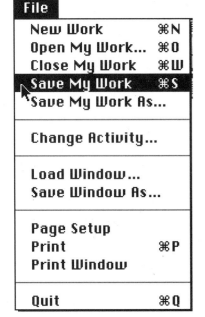

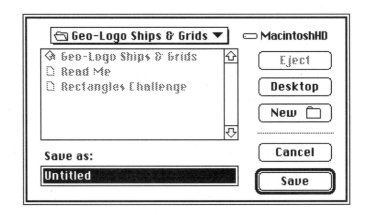

☞ 2. Press **<delete>** to erase **Untitled**.

☞ 3. **Type** a name for your work such as **GW Taxi 4/23**. (You can choose any name, but keep in mind that useful names include information that helps you find your work, such as your name, the activity, and the date. Spaces can be used in the titles of saved work.)

☞ 4. Click **[Save]**.

Notice that the name of your work now appears in the title bar of the Drawing window.

When you save your work this way, a copy is stored on the computer disk. You can shut off the computer and come back to this work at another time.

Open *Geo-Logo* and select **[Taxi]** (or whatever activity you choose) following the steps in Getting Started with *Geo-Logo* on p. 95.

How to Continue with Saved Work

☞ 1. **To continue** with work you saved previously—

a. **Choose Open My Work** from the **File** menu.

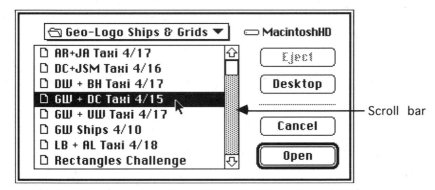

Scroll bar

If you saved your work on a different disk, insert that disk, click **[Desktop]**, and choose the disk from the menu.

b. **Select** your work by clicking on its **title**. If necessary, click the up or down arrows in the scroll bar or press the arrow keys to scroll up and down the list to find the title.

c. Click **[Open]**.

More About Taxi

The Tool window for Taxi:

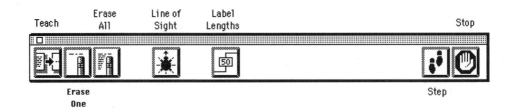

Teach   Erase All   Line of Sight   Label Lengths   Stop

Erase One   Step

Line of Sight   Draws an arrow to show the turtle's heading and rays for each 30°.

Label Lengths   Shows length of line segments in turtle steps on the Drawing window.

- For more details about these and other tools, see Tools on p. 124.

- Choose **Show Notes** from the **Windows** menu to record your thoughts and observations about your work.

- You can print an entire game, including the picture, list of commands, and procedures. Choose **Print** from the **File** menu.

- You can print a single window, showing either a list of your commands or a copy of your picture. Click that window and choose **Print Window** from the **File** menu.

Open *Geo-Logo* and select **[Bulletin Board]**, following steps 1 and 2 in Getting Started with *Geo-Logo* on p. 95.

A dialogue box appears with directions.

Click **[OK]**.

The object of Bulletin Board is to write *Geo-Logo* commands that the turtle follows to draw rectangles. In a later activity, you will place a rectangle in each quadrant of a coordinate grid.

 1. **Enter** move (fd or bk) and turn (lt or rt) **commands** to draw a rectangle. Make sure the turtle ends facing the same way it was when it started.

 2. **Change** the numbers in the commands to make a different rectangle.

(Remember to press **<return>** after you have typed or changed one or more commands and you are ready for the turtle to follow them. For the remainder of the tutorial, when directions say to enter a command or group of commands, it means type it in and press **<return>**.)

You may enjoy exploring *Geo-Logo* a bit more. For instance, try changing commands to make a square, a quadrilateral that is not a rectangle, or a quadrilateral that goes off the screen.

You may wish to use the **Label Lengths tool** 🔲 and the **Label Turns tool** 🔲 to double-check that opposite sides are the same length and turns are all 90°.

 3. **Teach** one of the rectangles in preparation for the next part, How to Make a Bulletin Board.

 4. **Erase All** and try your rectangle procedure. If you wish, make changes in the Teach window and rerun your rectangle procedure.

 5. **Pause and Reflect.** You might want to pause for a bit and reflect on your mathematical thinking in this activity. Here are some questions you might consider:

   - How did you know which commands to change to make a different rectangle?

   - How did you know which commands not to change?

   - How do *Geo-Logo* commands and patterns of commands reflect the geometric properties of rectangles?

   - How does writing commands to teach the turtle how to draw a rectangle help your thinking about the properties of rectangles? How might it help you think about defining a rectangle?

How to Make Rectangles

Draw and place pictures to make a bulletin board.

[OK]

How to Make a Bulletin Board

If necessary, write a procedure for a rectangle and Teach it following the steps in the last section, How to Make Rectangles.

☛ 1. **Run** the rectangle procedure you created in the last section.

The object of this activity is to place this rectangle in each of the four quadrants of the coordinate grid so you create a symmetrical bulletin board.

☛ 2. **Click** the **Grid tool** 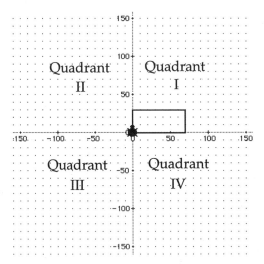 to show the initial location of the rectangle.

For example, if you used rt to draw your rectangle, it will appear in the lower-left corner of Quadrant I. If you used lt, your rectangle will appear in Quadrant II.

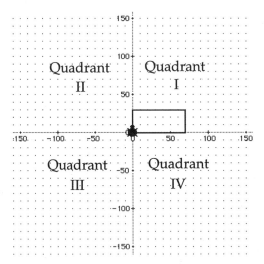

☛ 3. **Click** on **Erase All tool** to clear the screen.

You are now ready to place the rectangle in each of four quadrants to create a symmetrical bulletin board.

☛ 4. **Enter** a jumpto command followed by the procedure to place the rectangle in Quadrant I. It should not touch either axis.

☛ 5. **Enter** jumpto commands followed by the procedure to place the rectangle in each of the other quadrants so the bulletin board is symmetrical about both the vertical and horizontal axes.

(One way to check symmetry is to imagine folding the bulletin board along each of the axes to check whether the rectangles are the same distance away from that axis.)

☛ 6. **Teach** the commands in the Command Center as a procedure.

☛ 7. **Click** on **Erase All tool** and run your procedure to try it.

If your computer has color capability, try making your rectangles different colors by adding setc commands to the beginning of each procedure in the Teach window. For more information, see setc in Commands, p. 121.

☞ 8. **Print** your bulletin board, if possible. If the drawing window does not print completely, select "Color/Grayscale" in the Print dialog box.

☞ 9. **Pause and Reflect.** You might want to pause for a bit and reflect on your mathematical thinking in this activity. Here are some questions you might consider:

■ How did you figure out the coordinates for jumpto?

■ Did you find a pattern for the jumpto coordinates in various quadrants?

More About Bulletin Board

The Tool window for Bulletin Board:

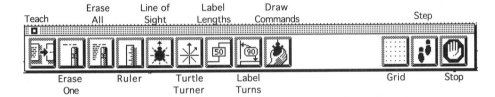

| | Ruler | Measures length, starting at the turtle's position. Click to freeze the ruler and show length. |

| | Turtle Turner | Measures turns from the turtle's heading. One arrowhead shows the turtle's heading. The other follows the cursor. Click to freeze and show turn. |

| | Label Turns | Labels the amount of each turtle turn in degrees. |

| | Draw Commands | Use the mouse to turn and move the turtle. Corresponding *Geo-Logo* commands are created automatically. |

| | Grid | Displays the coordinate plane with labeled axes on the drawing window. |

How to Make Pictures Using
rect

Use the rect procedure to make your picture.

[OK]

Open *Geo-Logo* and select **[Rectangle Pictures]**, following steps 1 and 2 in Getting Started with *Geo-Logo* on p. 95.

A dialogue box appears with directions.

Click **[OK]**.

The object of Rectangle Pictures is to use the procedure rect along with commands to draw and place rectangles to make various pictures.

The procedure rect is a shortcut for drawing rectangles that has already been entered and is available in this activity. When you use rect, the rectangles follow the same pattern of move and turn commands, with different numbers for the lengths of their sides.

The rect procedure contains the commands fd and rt and uses the variables L1 and L2 for side lengths.

```
to rect :L1 :L2
fd :L1
rt 90
fd :L2
rt 90
fd :L1
rt 90
fd :L2
rt 90
end
```

To use rect, choose side lengths by entering two numbers—for example, enter rect 30 50.

1. **Draw** a rectangle on the screen by entering rect 30 50 (or whatever lengths you want).

2. **Explore** the rect command a bit, entering rect commands with different side lengths.

3. **Click Erase All** 🖼 to clear the screen.

4. **Click Grid** ⬛ to display the coordinate grid.

5. **Enter** jumpto and rect commands to draw each of the pictures on the next page. One should be in Quadrant I, one in Quadrant II, and the third partly in Quadrant III and partly in Quadrant IV. Make the pictures any size but do not overlap them. Be sure to teach each procedure after you draw it.

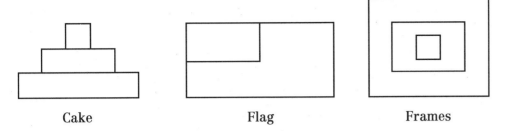

| Cake | Flag | Frames |

☛ 6. **Teach** your turtle this group of commands and procedures as a new procedure.

Enter one word to have the turtle draw all three shapes on the grid at the same time.

If you have a color or gray-scale monitor, add color to the pictures by adding a setc command to the beginning of each procedure. You might include setc commands while drawing pictures or add them later to procedures in the Teach window.

☛ 7. **Print** your finished pictures, if possible.

☛ 8. **Save** your work.

☛ 9. **Pause and Reflect.** You might want to pause for a bit and reflect on your mathematical thinking in this activity. Here are some questions you might consider:

- How does using the rect procedure help you think about rectangles?

- What mathematical thinking did you use to figure out the rectangle sizes and the jumpto numbers?

How to Turn and Repeat Rectangles

Open *Geo-Logo* and select **[Rectangle Pictures]**, following Steps 1 and 2 in Getting Started with *Geo-Logo* on p. 95. Click **[OK]** in the dialogue box. (The grid is not needed for this activity.)

The object of this activity is to draw rectangles in various orientations, then use the repeat command to explore rotations.

☛ 1. **Draw a rectangle** using the rect procedure. For example, enter rect 60 40.

☛ 2. **Click** 🖾 Erase All.

☞ 3. **Enter** the rect procedure again, but this time add a turn command on the same line before rect. For example, enter
rt 60 rect 60 40.

☞ 4. **Enter** the same set of commands two or three more times.

Notice that the rectangle rotates around a single point.

☞ 5. Click ⊞ **Erase All.**

☞ 6. Use the repeat command to explore this rotation. Follow these steps:

   a. Enter repeat __ [rt __ rect __ __] with numbers in each blank.

   b. Make changes to the numbers and rerun the command to see what happens.

   c. Find a repeat number to make the rectangle rotate all the way around.

☞ 7. Click ⊞ **Erase All.**

☞ 8. **Add** a move command to the list of commands inside the bracket. For example, repeat 4 [fd 100 rt 90 rect 40 60].

☞ 9. **Change** the **order** of commands inside the brackets and see what happens.

☞ 10. **Teach** (and print, if possible) any particularly interesting combinations.

☞ 11. **Pause and Reflect.** You might want to pause for a bit and reflect on your mathematical thinking in this activity. Here are some questions you might consider:

   ■ How did you figure out what combination of repeat numbers and turn commands was needed to rotate all the way around?

   ■ How does using the repeat command help you think about rotations and symmetry?

How to Make Rectangle Patterns

Open *Geo-Logo* and select **[Rectangle Pictures]**, following steps 1 and 2 in Getting Started with *Geo-Logo* on p. 95. Click **[OK]** in the dialogue box.

The object of this activity is to plan and draw complex patterns using only rectangles.

☛ 1. Choose **Hide Drawing** from the **Windows** menu.

☛ 2. **Enter** these commands: rect 100 10
                                    rect 90 20
                                    rect 80 30

plus two more that continue the same pattern

☛ 3. **Predict** what this will look like. You might want to sketch your ideas on paper.

☛ 4. Choose **Show Drawing** from the **Windows** menu and check your prediction.

☛ 5. **Explore** this pattern a bit. Try the following:

   a. Continue to enter rect commands to finish the pattern.

   b. Teach this procedure.

   c. To make another pattern, click **Erase All** and enter a repeat command that uses this pattern and a turn command. For example, repeat 4 [yourprocedurename rt 90].

☛ 6. **Teach** (and print, if possible) any interesting patterns.

☛ 7. **Pause and Reflect.** You might want to pause for a bit and reflect on your mathematical thinking in this activity. Here are some questions you might consider:

   ■ How does working with rect and repeat commands in *Geo-Logo* help your thinking about symmetry? About patterns? About geometric characteristics?

Design Your Own Rectangle Pattern

Open *Geo-Logo* and select **[Rectangle Pictures]**, following steps 1 and 2 in Getting Started with *Geo-Logo* on p. 95. Click **[OK]** in the dialogue box.

The object of this activity is to design a pattern, then plan how to draw it using the commands in this unit.

☛ 1. **Design** a rectangle pattern. You might want to sketch it on blank paper or use Student Sheet 13, Procedure Planning Paper (page 147).

☛ 2. **Plan** which *Geo-Logo* commands you will use to draw your design. Write these commands on paper first. Complete the entire plan before entering any commands on the computer.

Use any of the following *Geo-Logo* commands: fd, bk, rt, lt, rect, jumpto, repeat, and setc. Your plan might include procedures that you define and use within commands, such as repeat 3 [yourprocedurename rt 60].

☞ 3. **Enter** your commands to draw your design on the computer.

☞ 4. **Teach** your design as a procedure so you can draw the entire design using only one command. Print your design, if possible.

☞ 5. **Plan** and draw another pattern without writing the commands on paper first. Teach it as a procedure and print it.

☞ 6. **Save** your work.

☞ 7. **Pause and Reflect.** You might want to pause for a bit and reflect on your mathematical thinking in this activity. Here are some questions you might consider:

  ■ How was what you planned on paper different from what your finished computer drawing looked like?

  ■ How is your thinking different when you plan something on paper before trying it on the computer?

More About Rectangle Pictures

The Tool window for Rectangle Pictures:

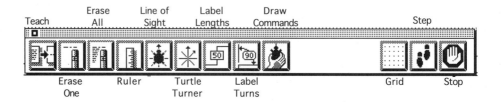

All tools have been described in earlier sections. For more information, see Tools, p. 124.

Free Explore

The Free Explore activity is available for you to use to extend and enhance activities in the unit and as an environment to further explore *Geo-Logo*.

In Free Explore, the turtle responds to all *Geo-Logo* commands and all tools are available from the Tool window.

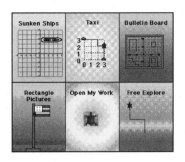

Various shapes, some rectangles and some not, are drawn and saved as procedures in the file named Rectangles Challenge. You might find these useful for extending class discussion about the properties of rectangles. To view these shapes, follow these steps:

Open *Geo-Logo* and select **[Free Explore]**, following steps 1 and 2 in Getting Started with *Geo-Logo* on p. 95.

☞ 1. From the **File** menu, choose **Open My Work**.

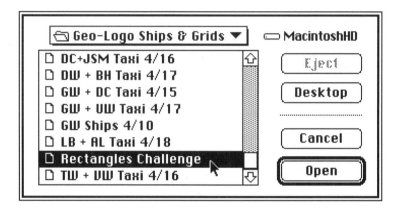

☞ 2. **Double-click** to select **Rectangles Challenge** from the menu in the dialogue box.

☞ 3. Type **s1** and press **<return>** to view the first shape for discussion.

☞ 4. **Discuss** whether the shape is a rectangle. Suggest to students that they ask themselves if the shape has all the properties of rectangles (for example, four straight sides; opposite sides equal; opposite sides parallel; four equal angles produced by 90° turns; simple closed figure).

☞ 5. **Show** students how to use the **Label Lengths** and **Label Turn tools** to check that the opposite sides are the same length and that the turns are all 90°. **Turn off these tools** to get ready for the next shape.

☞ 6. Click Erase All to clear the screen.

☞ 7. **Continue** to type **s2** through **s10**, clearing the screen between each, to view the other shapes.

Help

Assistance is available as you work with *Geo-Logo* activities. From the **Help** menu, choose any of the following:

Windows provides information on *Geo-Logo*'s three main windows: Command Center, Drawing, and Teach.

Vocabulary provides a listing of *Geo-Logo*'s commands and examples.

Tools provides information on *Geo-Logo*'s tools (represented on the Tools window as icons).

Directions provides instructions for the present activity.

Hints gives a series of hints on the present activity, one at a time. It is dimmed when there are no available hints.

The Coordinate Grid

The turtle's location in the Drawing window can be described as a position on a coordinate grid with the origin [0 0] in the middle of the screen where the turtle starts. The tool to display this grid is available in the Tool window in some activities.

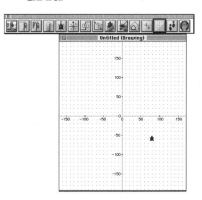

In *Geo-Logo*, locations on this grid are described using two numbers, without a comma, within square brackets. For example, the turtle in this picture is at [80 –60]. Commands such as jumpto [80 –60] use coordinates for locations.

Commands

The following commands are available in *Geo-Logo*. Some have been previously introduced in the investigations where they are most useful.

Command	What It Means	What It Does
bk 10	back 10	Moves the turtle back 10 steps (use whatever number you wish). The turtle leaves a path if its pen is down. *See also* pd *and* pu.

Command	What It Means	What It Does
ct	clear text	Clears, or erases, all the text in the Print window.
eraseall	erase all	Erases all the commands in the Command Center.
fd 50	forward 50	Moves the turtle forward 50 steps (use whatever number you wish). *See also* pd *and* pu.
fill	fill	Fills a closed shape or the entire Drawing window with the current turtle's color, starting at the current turtle's position. If the turtle's pen is over a path, only that path is filled. To fill a shape, use pu, then fd and rt or lt to move inside the shape; use setc to set the color, then fill. **Note**: If the shape you want to fill is on a grid, turn off the grid first before filling. Use the hp command to hide points if you want to use jumpto with fill.
hp	hide points	Hides points (they become invisible).
ht	hide turtle	Hides the current turtle (it becomes invisible).
jumpto [__ __]		Moves the turtle to the point whose coordinates are in the bracket without drawing a path. You can use jt as abbreviation for jumpto.
jumpto A		Moves the turtle to point A without drawing a path. The point must already have been defined with that letter.
lt 120	left 120	Turns the turtle left 120 (or any number of) degrees.
make-points [A [20 50] B [-70 -100]]		Makes points and shows them on the Drawing window. See the **Make Points tool**, which automatically generates this command. (See p. 124.)
pd	pen down	Puts the turtle's pen down so that when it moves, it draws a path.

Command	What It Means	What It Does
print [My drawing]		Prints whatever is within brackets or acts as a calculator. For example, if you type pr 85 + 15, *Geo-Logo* will print 100.
print colors		Prints a list of colors available to use with the setc command.
pu	pen up	Puts the turtle's pen up so that when it moves, it does not leave a path (it does not draw).
repeat 4 [fd 10 rt 90]		Repeats the commands in the list the specified number of times—in this example, four times. (The "list" is whatever is between the [square brackets].)
rt 45	right 45	Turns the turtle right 45 degrees (or any number of degrees).
setc black	set color	Sets the turtle's color; this affects the color of the turtle and the color for drawing and filling. The color names are: white black gray gray2 yellow orange red pink violet blue blue2 green green2 brown brown2 gray3.
sp	show points	Shows points and labels.
st	show turtle	Shows the turtle.

Other Commands and the Active Procedure

Choose **Vocabulary** on the **Help** menu to get information about other *Geo-Logo* commands.

Several of these commands, such as the motions commands, are performed only on the "active" procedure—the last procedure (defined in the Teach window) that has been run in the Command Center. To activate any other procedure, click on it in the Drawing window.

Menus

How to Use Menus

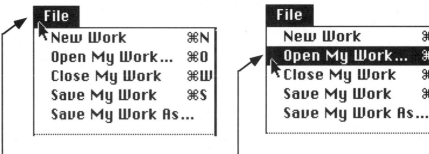

Point to the menu you want and press the mouse button...

...then drag the selection bar to your choice and release the button

Some menu choices are also available from the keyboard. On the menu, the ⌘N indicates that, instead of selecting the choice from the menu, you could type ⌘-N. Hold down the Command key (with the ⌘ and symbols on it) then press the **<N>** key.

A menu choice may be dimmed indicating it is not available in a particular situation. For example, **Undo** is not available in this case.

Geo-Logo's Menus

The **File** menu deals with documents and quitting.

> **New Work** starts a new document.
>
> **Open My Work** opens previously saved work.
>
> **Close My Work** closes present work.
>
> **Save My Work** saves the work.
>
> **Save My Work As** saves the work with a new name or in a new location.
>
> **Page Setup** allows changes to printing options.
>
> **Print** prints a whole document.
>
> **Print Window** prints only the active window (the last one clicked on).
>
> **Quit** quits *Geo-Logo*.

The **Edit** menu contains choices to use when editing your work:

Undo reverses the last thing done, such as **Delete**, **Cut**, **Erase**, and **Erase All**.

Cut deletes the selected object and saves it to a space called the clipboard.

Copy copies selected object to the clipboard.

Paste places the contents of the clipboard in the cursor location.

Clear deletes the selected object (works the same as using the **<delete>** key).

Stopall stops running this procedure.

The **Font** menu is used to change the appearance of text. The change applies to the active window (Command Center, Teach, Print, or Notes windows).

The first names are choices of typeface.

Size and **Style** have additional choices; pull down to select them and then to the right.

For **Style**, the choices are listed to the right. Continue to hold the mouse button and move the cursor to highlight one of them.

The **Size** choice works the same way.

All Large changes all text in all windows to a large-size font. This is useful for demonstrations. Once selected, it toggles (changes back and forth) to **All Small**.

The **Windows** menu shows or hides the windows. If you hide the Drawing window, the menu item changes to **Show Drawing**. You can also hide a window by clicking in the "close box" in the upper-left corner of the window.

Show Print opens the Print window and displays text generated by a print command from the Command Center. The Notes window (initially hidden) can be used to enter and keep more permanent notes.

The **Options** menu allows you to customize *Geo-Logo*.

Fast Turtle turns the turtle quickly and so speeds up drawing. Usually in *Geo-Logo*, the turtle turns slowly, to help students build images of the turns.

Turn Rays displays rays during turns to help visualize the turn. After a turn command is entered, a ray is drawn to show the turtle's initial heading. Then as the turtle turns, another ray turns with it, showing the change in heading throughout the turn. A ray also marks every 30° of turn.

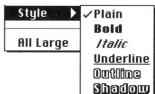

Decimal Places ▸ ✓0
Scale Distance... | 1
| 2

Decimal Places controls how many numbers after the decimal point (i.e., 10ths, 100ths...) are printed by certain commands and tools, such as the **Ruler**, **Turtle Turner**, **Label Lines**, and **Label Turns tools**. If 0 (zero) numbers are shown, the number is rounded to the nearest integer.

The **Help** menu provides assistance.

Help
Windows...
Vocabulary...
Tools...
Directions... ⌘D
Hints... ⌘H

Windows provides information on *Geo-Logo*'s three main windows: Command Center, Drawing, and Teach.

Vocabulary provides a list of *Geo-Logo*'s commands.

Tools provides information on *Geo-Logo*'s tools (represented on the Tools window as icons).

Directions provides instructions for the present activity.

Hints gives a series of hints on the present activity, one at a time. It is dimmed when there are no available hints.

Tools

Only the most commonly used tools are available and displayed for each activity. All tools are available for Free Explore.

Click on a tool to use it.

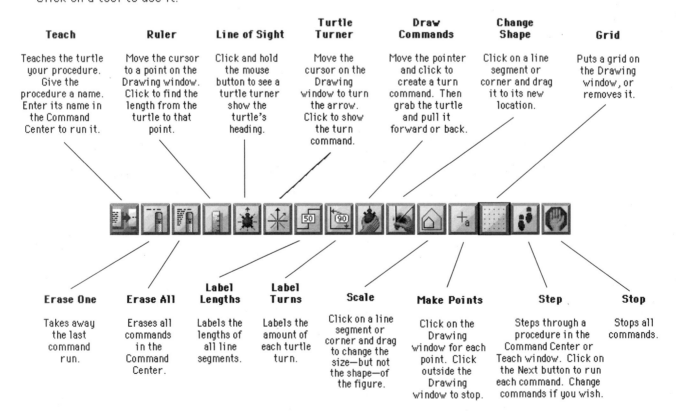

Teach
Teaches the turtle your procedure. Give the procedure a name. Enter its name in the Command Center to run it.

Ruler
Move the cursor to a point on the Drawing window. Click to find the length from the turtle to that point.

Line of Sight
Click and hold the mouse button to see a turtle turner show the turtle's heading.

Turtle Turner
Move the cursor on the Drawing window to turn the arrow. Click to show the turn command.

Draw Commands
Move the pointer and click to create a turn command. Then grab the turtle and pull it forward or back.

Change Shape
Click on a line segment or corner and drag it to its new location.

Grid
Puts a grid on the Drawing window, or removes it.

Erase One
Takes away the last command run.

Erase All
Erases all commands in the Command Center.

Label Lengths
Labels the lengths of all line segments.

Label Turns
Labels the amount of each turtle turn.

Scale
Click on a line segment or corner and drag to change the size—but not the shape—of the figure.

Make Points
Click on the Drawing window for each point. Click outside the Drawing window to stop.

Step
Steps through a procedure in the Command Center or Teach window. Click on the Next button to run each command. Change commands if you wish.

Stop
Stops all commands.

The *Geo-Logo* screen looks like this:

Pull down to choose menus.

Click to choose a tool.

File Edit Font Windows Options Help

Command Center
```
pu fd 80
pd
fd 40
square
```

Untitled (Drawing)

Teach
```
to square
fd 20
rt 90
fd 20
rt 90
fd 20
rt 90
fd 20
rt 90
end
```

Type commands in the Command Center. Press RETURN or ENTER to run them.

The turtle draws in the Drawing window.

Defined procedures go in the Teach window.

Command Center

Type commands you wish the turtle to run immediately in the Command Center. Press the **<return>** key after each command. Make changes to commands directly in the Command Center; they are reflected automatically in the drawing when you press **<return>**. If you need to insert a line, hold down the **<command>** key and press the **<L>** key.

Teach Window

When you have a sequence of commands you might wish to use again, you can make it a procedure. Click the **Teach tool** . A dialogue box appears, asking for a one-word name for the procedure. The name (with the word *to* in front of it) and the commands (with *end* added) are placed in the Teach window on the right and named as a defined, or taught, procedure. You can then type the name of the procedure as a new command.

If you change a procedure in the Teach window (for example, changing each fd 20 to fd 30 in the procedure square above), the change will be reflected in the Drawing window as soon as you click out of the Teach window.

This section contains suggestions for how to correct errors, how to get back to what you want to be doing when you are somewhere else in the program, and what to do in some troubling situations.

If you are new to using the computer, you might also ask a computer coordinator or an experienced friend for help.

No *Geo-Logo* Icon to Open

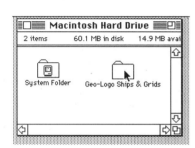

- Check that *Geo-Logo* Ships & Grids has been installed on your computer by looking at a listing of the hard disk.

- Open the folder labeled *Geo-Logo* Ships & Grids by double-clicking on it.

- Find the icon for the *Geo-Logo* Ships & Grids application and double-click on it.

Geo-Logo Ships & Grids

Nothing Happened After Double-Clicking on the *Geo-Logo* Icon

- If you are sure you double-clicked correctly, wait a bit longer. *Geo-Logo* takes a while to open or load and nothing new will appear on the screen for a few seconds.

- On the other hand, you may have double-clicked too slowly or moved the mouse between your clicks. In that case, try again.

In Wrong Activity

- Choose **Change Activity** from the **File** menu.

Text Written in Wrong Area

- Delete text.

- Click cursor in the desired area or on the desired line and retype text (or select text and use **Cut** and **Paste** from the **Edit** menu to move text to desired area).

Out of Room in Command Center

- Continue to enter commands. Text will scroll up and old commands will still be there but temporarily out of view. To scroll, click on the up or down arrows in the scroll bar along the right side of the window.

A Window Closed by Mistake

- Choose **Show Window** from the **Windows** menu.

Windows or Tools Dragged to a Different Position by Mistake

- Drag the window back into place by following these steps: Place the pointer arrow in the stripes of the title bar. Press and hold the button as you move the mouse. An outline of the window indicates the new location. Release the button and the window moves to that location.

I Clicked Somewhere and Now *Geo-Logo* Is Gone! What Happened?

You probably clicked in a part of the screen not used by *Geo-Logo*, and the computer therefore took you to another application, such as the "desktop."

- Click on a *Geo-Logo* window, if visible.

- Double-click on the *Geo-Logo* Ships & Grids program icon.

The Turtle Disappeared off the Screen. Why?

- If a command moves the turtle off the screen, write the opposite command to make it return. For example, if fd 500 sent the turtle off the screen, bk 500 will return it.

  Note: Many versions of Logo "wrap"—that is, when the turtle is sent off the top of the screen, it reappears from the bottom. *Geo-Logo* does not wrap when it is opened because students are learning to connect *Geo-Logo* commands to the geometric figures they draw.

How Do I Select a Section of Text?

In certain situations, you may copy or delete a section, or block, of text.

- Point and click at one end of the text. Drag the mouse by holding down the mouse button as you move to the other end of the text. Release the mouse button. Then use the **Edit** menu to **Copy**, **Cut**, and **Paste**.

System Error Message

- Some difficulty with the *Geo-Logo* program or your computer caused the computer to stop functioning. Turn off the computer and repeat the steps to turn it on and start *Geo-Logo* again. Any work you saved will still be available to open from your disk.

I Tried to Print and Nothing Happened.

- Check that the printer is connected and turned on and that "Color/Grayscale" is selected in the Print dialog box.

- When printers are not functioning properly, a system error may occur causing the computer to "freeze." If there is no response from the keyboard or when moving or clicking with the mouse, you may have to shut down the computer and start over.

The turtle responds to *Geo-Logo* commands as a robot. If it does not understand a command or has a suggestion, a dialogue box may appear with one of the following messages. Read the message, click on **[OK]** or press **<return>** from the keyboard and correct the situation as needed.

Disk or directory full.

>The computer disk is full.

>■ Use **Save My Work As** to choose a different disk.

I don't know how to *name*.

>Program does not recognize the command as written.

>| | |
>|---|---|
>| fd50 | needs a space between fd and 50 –> fd 50 |
>| fdd 50 | extra d |
>| mypicturje | misspelling |

I don't know what to do with *name*.

>You may have given too many inputs to a command or no command.

>| | |
>|---|---|
>| fd 50 30 | needs only one number |

>You may have left out a command.

>| | |
>|---|---|
>| 5 + 16 | change to print 5 + 16 |

I'm having trouble with the disk or drive.

>The disk might be write-protected, there is no disk in the drive, or some similar problem.

>■ Use **Save My Work As** to choose a different disk.

***Name* can only be used in a procedure.**

>Certain commands, such as end and stop, can't be used in the command center.

>■ Don't use that command if you don't need to.

>■ Define the procedure in the Teach window.

Name does not like *name* as input.

A command needs a certain type of input and didn't get it from the command following it.

fd fd 30   Omit one fd or put a number after the first one.

repeat [fd 30 rt 90]   repeat needs two inputs; a number and a list—for example, repeat 4 [fd 30 rt 90].

Name is already used.

A procedure already exists with that name.

■ Use a different name.

Name needs more inputs.

Command name needs an input, such as a number.

fd	Needs how much to move –> fd 30
rt	Needs how much to turn –> rt 30
rect	Needs length of sides –> rect 60 40
rect [60 40]	Needs numbers without bracket –> rect 60 40

Number too big

There are limits to numbers *Geo-Logo* can use; it can use numbers up to 2147483647.

■ Don't exceed the limit.

Out of space

There is no free memory left in the computer.

■ Enter the command recycle to clean up and reorganize available memory.

■ Eliminate commands or procedures you don't need.

■ Save and start new work.

The maximum *value* for *name* is *number.*

The input is too high.

For example, The maximum value for fd is 9999.

■ Use a smaller number.

The minimum *value* for *name* is *number.*

The input is too low a number.

For example, The minimum value for fd is -9999.

■ Use a higher number.

The *Geo-Logo* disk for *Sunken Ships and Grids Patterns* that you received with this unit contains the *Geo-Logo* Ships & Grids program, a Read Me file, and Rectangles Challenge. You may run the program directly from this disk, but it is better to put a copy of the program and files on your hard disk and store the original disk for safekeeping. Putting a program on your hard disk is called *installing* it.

Note: *Geo-Logo* runs on an Macintosh II computer or above, with 4 MB of internal memory (RAM) and Apple System Software 7.0 or later. (*Geo-Logo* can run on a Macintosh with less internal memory, but the system software must be configured to use a minimum of memory.)

slide tab up
to lock   Back of disk

To install the contents of the *Geo-Logo* Ships & Grids disk on your hard drive, follow the instructions for your type of computer or these steps:

1. Lock the *Geo-Logo* Ships & Grids program disk by sliding up the black tab on the back, so the hole is open.

   The *Geo-Logo* Ships & Grids disk is your master copy. Locking the disk allows copying while protecting its contents.

2. Insert the *Geo-Logo* Ships & Grids disk into the floppy disk drive.

3. Double-click the icon of the *Geo-Logo* Ships & Grids disk to open it.

4. Double-click on the Read Me file to open and read it for any recent changes in how to install or use *Geo-Logo*. Click in the close box after reading.

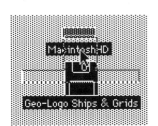

5. Click on and drag the *Geo-Logo* Ships & Grids disk icon (the outline moves) to the hard disk icon until the hard disk icon is highlighted, then release the mouse button.

   A message appears indicating that the contents of the *Geo-Logo* Ships & Grids disk are being copied to the hard disk. The copy is in a folder on the hard disk with the name *Geo-Logo* Ships & Grids.

6. Eject the *Geo-Logo* Ships & Grids disk by dragging it to the trash. Store the disk in a safe place.

7. If the hard disk window is not open on the desktop, open the hard disk by double-clicking on the icon.

   When you open the hard disk icon, the hard disk window appears, showing you the contents of your hard disk. Among its contents is the folder labeled *Geo-Logo* Ships & Grids holding the contents of the *Geo-Logo* disk.

☛ 8. Double-click the *Geo-Logo* Ships & Grids folder to select and open it.

When you open the *Geo-Logo* Ships & Grids folder, the window contains the program for this unit.

To select and run *Geo-Logo* Ships & Grids, double-click on the program icon.

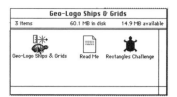

For ease at startup, you might create an alias for the *Geo-Logo* Ships & Grids program by following these steps:

Optional

☛ 1. Select the program icon.

☛ 2. Choose **Make Alias** from the **File** menu.

The alias is connected to the original file that it represents, so when you open an alias, you are actually opening the original file. This alias can be moved to any location on the desktop.

☛ 3. Move the *Geo-Logo* Ships & Grids alias out of the window to the desktop space under the hard disk icon.

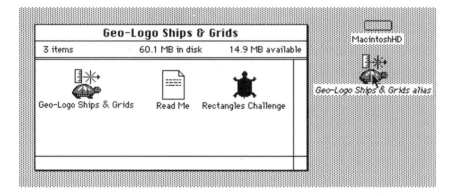

For startup, double-click on the *Geo-Logo* Ships & Grids alias instead of opening the *Geo-Logo* Ships & Grids folder to start the program inside.

Saving Work on a Different Disk

For classroom management purposes, you might want to save student work on a disk other than the program disk or hard disk. Make sure the save-to disk has been initialized (see instructions for your computer system).

☞ 1. Insert the save-to disk into the drive.

☞ 2. Choose **Save My Work As** from the **File** menu.

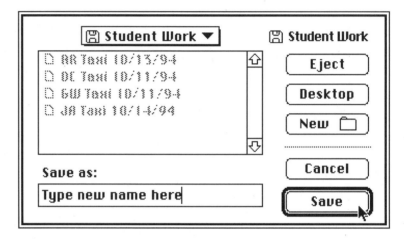

The name of the disk the computer is saving to is displayed in the dialogue box. To choose a different disk, click the **[Desktop]** button and double-click to choose and open a disk from the new menu.

☞ 3. Type a name for your work if you want it to have a new or different name from the one it currently has.

☞ 4. Click on **[Save]**.

Deleting Copies of Student Work

As students no longer need previously saved work, you may want to delete their work (called "files") from a disk. This cannot be accomplished from inside the *Geo-Logo* program. However, you can delete files from disks at any time by following directions for how to "Delete a File" for your computer system.

Blackline Masters

_____ , 19 ____

Dear Family,

Our class is beginning a new mathematics unit called *Sunken Ships and Grid Patterns*. This unit introduces an important part of geometry: naming and locating points on a grid. Finding and plotting points and labeling them with their location or coordinates are things students will do in math from now through high school.

In this unit, we introduce the idea of plotting a point through the fanciful context of Grid City. Students will move a "taxicab" through the city to think about locations and distances on a grid. To put together their knowledge of coordinates and distances, students will then play a game called Sunken Ships, where the goal is to find each other's ships quickly. Students will also create coordinate mysteries for one another. These are connect-the-dot pictures, where each dot is specified by grid points or coordinates.

In the second half of this unit, students use the computer language *Geo-Logo* to explore the characteristics of rectangles. They investigate symmetry by making symmetrical "bulletin boards" of rectangles. As a final project, students create designs that look complicated but are easy to make on the computer using *Geo-Logo*. We hope you will enjoy seeing these beautiful and mathematically interesting designs.

During this unit, you can help by:

- Offering to solve your child's coordinate mystery after he or she creates it. If you are unsure of how to read grid coordinates, your child can help you.
- Playing Sunken Ships with your child when he or she brings it home. Your child can teach you the rules—and maybe even some good strategies!
- Keep your eyes open for rectangles in the world around you—they're easy to spot. Work with your child to find particularly large or small (smaller than an inch on a side) rectangles, rectangles that are also squares (all sides are equal), and rectangles that are much taller than most fourth graders.

Thank you for your continuing interest in your child's mathematics work.

Sincerely,

Grid City

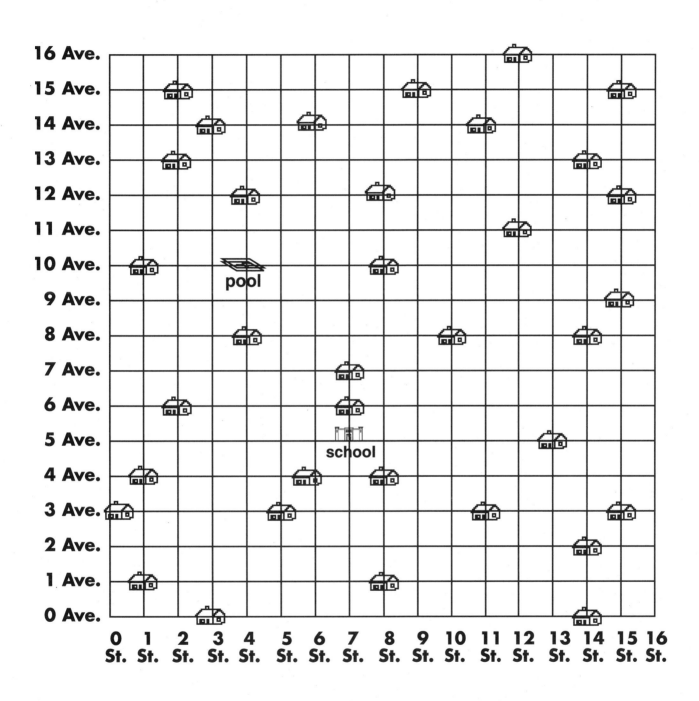

Finding Distances in Grid City

1. What are the coordinates of your house? _____

The coordinates of the school are (7, 5).

How many blocks is your house from the school? _____

2. Who is your partner? _____

What are the coordinates of your partner's house? _____

How many blocks is your house from your partner's house?

_____

3. Whose house is closest to yours? _____

How many blocks is your house from that house? _____

4. Whose house is farthest from yours? _____

How many blocks is that house from your house? _____

5. How many houses are less than 8 blocks from the school?

_____

Whose houses are they? _____

6. Who lives more than 16 blocks from the school?

_____

Coordinate Mystery

What is the mystery dot-to-dot picture?

Draw it by connecting the coordinates.

Start at this point:

(9,6)

Then draw straight line segments to each of these points in order:

(1, 6)   (8, 1)   (5, 9)   (2, 1)   (9, 6)

Your lines can go diagonally on the grid.

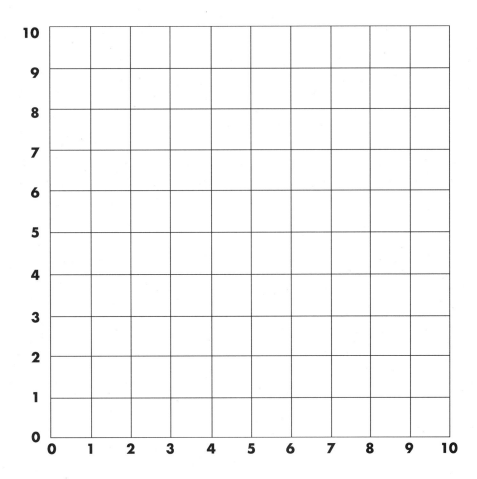

Four-Quadrant City Map

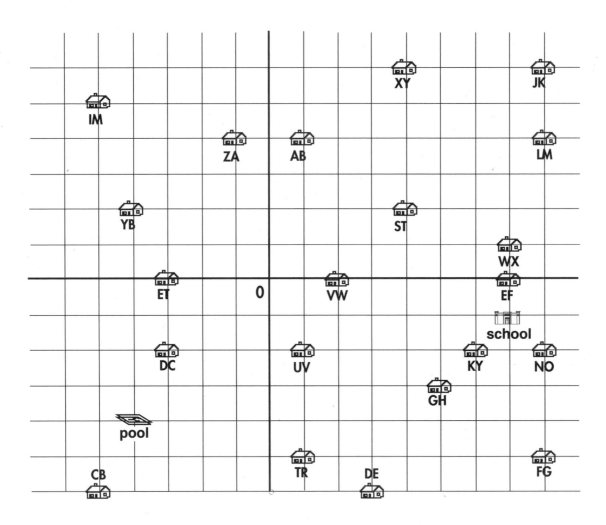

1. Label both axes with positive and negative numbers.

2. Put a park on the map fewer than 4 blocks from the school.

3. Put a store on the map more than 8 blocks from the school.

4. Find a place for a tennis court that is 2 blocks from the park and more than 2 blocks from the pool.

5. Put a high school on the map so it is at least 10 blocks from the school.

6. Place a video store less than 2 blocks from the pool.

Grid Paper

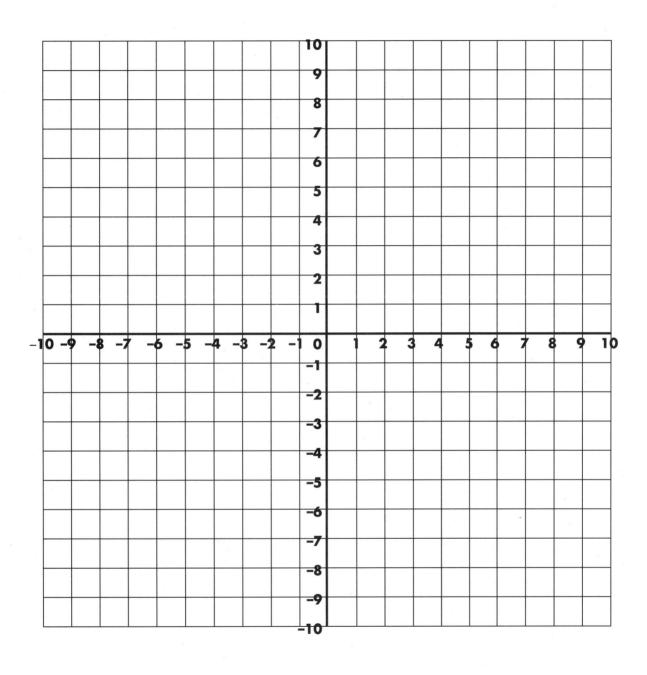

How to Play Sunken Ships on Paper

Two teams try to locate each other's sunken ships.

Setting up: Each team secretly draws a sunken ship on the grid labeled "Our Ship" on the Sunken Ships Grids sheet. Ships must cover five grid intersections lying on a vertical or horizontal straight line.

1. To begin, the first team decides where it wants to start its search for the other team's ship by naming a point, such as (–3, 5).

2. The second team checks to see if that point is on its ship. If it is, it says "Ship." If not, it gives the number of units to the nearest undiscovered point on the ship.

3. The first team records its point on the grid labeled "Their Ship." They write *S* for ship, if it is a point on the ship. Or they write the number indicating how many units away from the second team's ship their point is.

4. Then the second team guesses where to start its search for the first team's ship and names a point.

5. Teams take turns guessing points until they have *both* found all five points of the other's ship.

Number of turns it took us to find their sunken ship:	Number of turns it took them to find our sunken ship:
Round 1: _____	Round 1: _____
Round 2: _____	Round 2: _____
Round 3: _____	Round 3: _____

Sunken Ships Grids

Our Ship

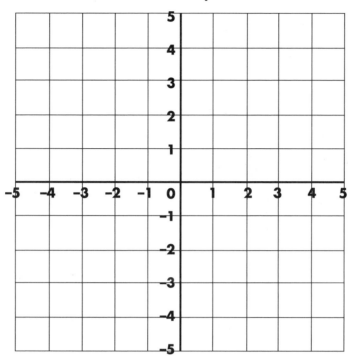

Their Ship

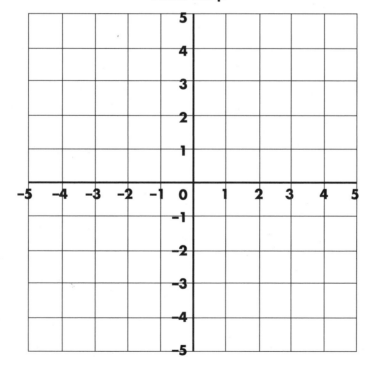

How to Play Sunken Ships on the Computer

1. Open *Geo-Logo* and choose Sunken Ship.

2. Type `hideship` and press **<return>** to tell the computer to draw a grid and hide a ship. The ship is 5 intersection points long.

3. Enter `jumpto` commands like `jumpto [-2 3]`. Each time you jump to a location, the computer tells you whether that point is on the ship. If it is, it prints *S* on the screen. If it is not, it prints how far away that point is from the nearest undiscovered point on the ship.

4. Continue to enter `jumpto` commands until you find all five points of the sunken ship. When you do, a ship appears on the screen. Keep track of the number of `jumpto` commands you needed below.

Number of `jumpto`'s to find the sunken ship:

Round 1: _____

Round 2: _____

Round 3: _____

Round 4: _____

Round 5: _____

Round 6: _____

Round 7: _____

Round 8: _____

Patterns in Paths

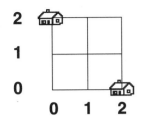

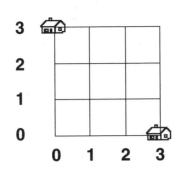

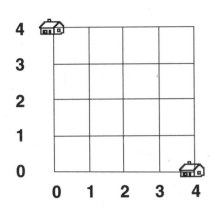

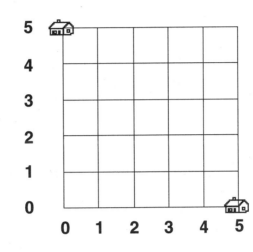

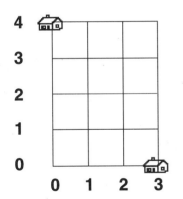

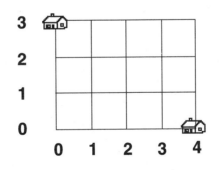

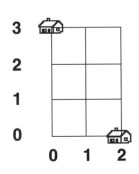

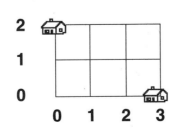

Rows	Columns	Blocks in Shortest Path
2	2	
3	3	
4	4	
5	5	
6	6	
7	7	
50	50	
4	3	
3	4	
3	2	
2	3	
7	8	
50	51	

Taxi

Teach the turtle taxi to drive along the shortest path that will go to each of the 5 houses and then back to the beginning.

1. On the computer, type map and press the **<return>** key.

2. Type the commands to make the turtle taxi drive to each house. Each block is 10 turtle steps long. Press **<return>** after each one.

3. Use the **Label Lengths tool** ⬛ to help you find the total length of the path.

4. Click the **Teach tool** ⬛ and name your procedure.

5. Run your procedure by entering its name in the Command Center, followed by **<return>**.

6. Erase the procedure with the **Erase All tool** ⬛. Try to make a shorter path. Make a new path by typing map and pressing the **<return>** key. Enter your new commands.

7. Record the length of the shortest path that goes to all five houses and back to the beginning.

    Total Length: _____ turtle steps

8. Draw your shortest path below.

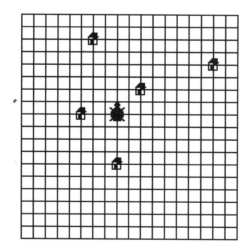

Distances and Coordinates

Find the shortest distance between these pairs of points. You may use the grid below to draw the points and find the distance between them. Try to find some ways to figure out the shortest distances without drawing lines between the points on the grid.

(0, 0) and (0, 30) _____

(0, 0) and (40, 0) _____

(20, 30) and (20, 0) _____

(0, 50) and (60, 50) _____

(30, 40) and (10, 40) _____

(50, 10) and (50, 50) _____

(30, 60) and (20, 60) _____

(20, 50) and (30, 40) _____

(50, 20) and (40, 30) _____

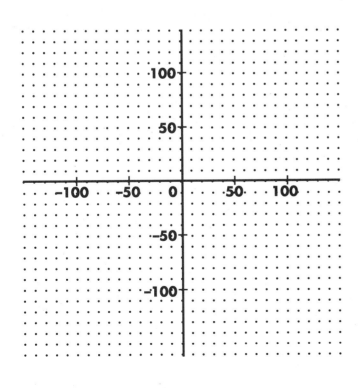

Designing a Town

Design a town so the statements below are true. Use one of the grids on Student Sheet 13 to make your map. Make sure you mark each place so you know what is there.

1. There is a City Hall at (−20, −20).

2. There are 8 houses. Two are in each quadrant. Make your house the one that is closest to City Hall. Mark it with your initials. What are the coordinates of your house? _____

3. There are two parks. The distance of one from City Hall is 30 steps. Another is just 10 steps from a house. What are the coordinates of the parks?

   Park 1 _____   Park 2 _____

4. There is a swimming pool 20 steps from one park. At what coordinates did you put the swimming pool?

   _____

5. There is a movie theater that is the same distance from City Hall as it is from the swimming pool. What are its coordinates? _____

6. Find a place for a school that is less than 20 steps from at least 3 houses. Where could it go?

   _____

   What are the coordinates of the 3 houses that are less than 20 steps away?

   House 1 _____   House 2 _____   House 3 _____

On a separate sheet of paper, write about how you decided where to put the pool and the school.

Procedure Planning Paper

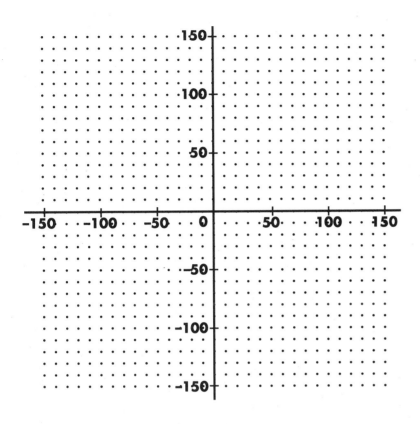

Commands

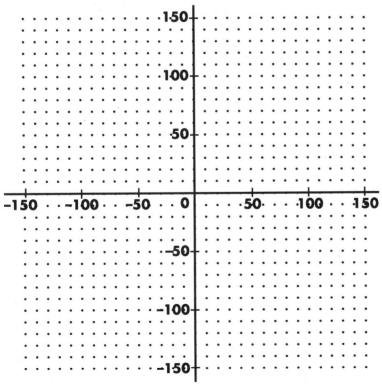

Commands

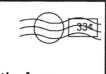
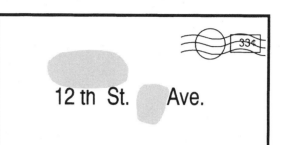

12 tn St. 11 th Ave.

12 th St. ___ Ave.

___ St. ___ Ave.

___ St. ___ Ave.

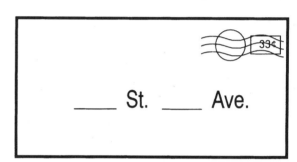
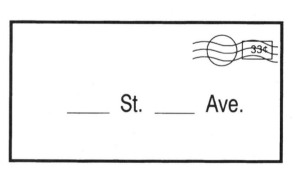

___ St. ___ Ave.

___ St. ___ Ave.

___ St. ___ Ave.

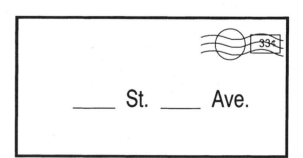

___ St. ___ Ave.

Investigation 1 • Resource
Sunken Ships and Grid Patterns

How to Get Started

- Turn on the computer.
- Open *Geo-Logo* with a double-click on the icon. Single-click on the opening screen.
- Single-click an activity button.

Geo-Logo Ships & Grids

Geo-Logo Commands

fd 50	moves forward 50 turtle steps
bk 120	moves back 120 turtle steps
lt 90	turns left 90 degrees
rt 60	turns right 60 degrees

setc red	sets the color to red
jumpto [30 40]	moves turtle to (30, 40)
repeat 4 [fd 40 rt 90]	repeats the command in brackets 4 times

---

Tools

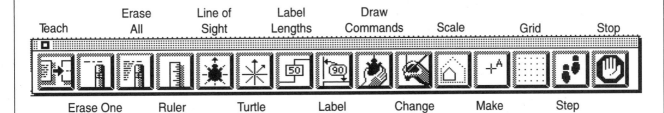

Teach — Erase All — Line of Sight — Label Lengths — Draw Commands — Scale — Grid — Stop

Erase One — Ruler — Turtle Turner — Label Turns — Change Shape — Make Points — Step

---

How to Get Help from *Geo-Logo*

- Choose a topic from the **Help** Menu.

How to Open Saved Work

- Turn on the computer, open *Geo-Logo*, select an activity.
- Choose **Open My Work** from the **File** menu.
- Click the name of your work.
- Click [Open].

How to Save Your Work

- Choose **Save My Work** from the **File** menu.
- First time, type a name like **DC+GW taxi 3/23**.
- Click [Save].

How to Finish

- Finish activity: Choose **Close My Work** from the **File** menu.
  STOP HERE if changing users.
- Finish *Geo-Logo*: Choose **Quit** from the **File** menu.
- Shut down and turn off the computer.

Finding Rectangles in the Room

Use a ruler, yardstick, or string, and a right-angle tester to find rectangles that meet the following conditions.

1. Find in the room a rectangle where two of the sides are about twice as long as the other two sides. What is it? Where is it? About how long are its sides?

2. Find in the room a rectangle where two of the sides are about four times as long as the other two sides. What is it? Where is it? About how long are its sides?

3. Find in the room a rectangle where two of the sides are about the same length as the other two sides. What is it? Where is it? About how long are its sides?

4. What is the largest rectangle you can find in the room? What is it? Where is it? About how long are its sides?

5. What is the smallest rectangle you can find in the room? What is it? Where is it? About how long are its sides?

Finding Rectangles in the Drawing

Outline in blue all the shapes in the drawing that are
rectangles. Outline in green all the shapes that are
rectangles in the real world but are not rectangles in
the drawing. Outline other shapes in red.

Finding Rectangles on the Grid

Which sets of the following coordinates form rectangles?
How do you know? Test each set by drawing the figures on
a piece of Procedure Planning Paper, connecting the points
in order, and returning to the starting point.

Figure A   Is it a rectangle?

(50, 130) (110, 130) (110, 100) (50, 100)

How do you know?

Figure B   Is it a rectangle?

(–110, –50) (–110, –70) (–90, –70) (–90, –50)

How do you know?

Figure C   Is it a rectangle?

(50, 50) (60, 70) (110, 70) (100, 50)

How do you know?

Figure D   Is it a rectangle?

(10, –100) (50, –60) (20, –30) (–20, –70)

How do you know?

Name ______________________ Date ______________

Student Sheet 17

Finding the Fourth Coordinate of Rectangles

For each of the following figures, find the fourth coordinate. When the points are connected in order (returning to the starting point), they should form a rectangle. Use a piece of Procedure Planning Paper to work on the rectangles.

First Three Coordinates	Fourth Coordinate
Figure A (50, 40) (50, 110) (70, 110)	
Figure B (–30, –70) (–30, –30) (10, –30)	
Figure C (–90, –110) (80, –110) (80, –80)	
Figure D (special challenge) (80, 50) (110, 80) (130, 60)	
Figure E (special challenge) (–80, 120) (–120, 80) (–80, 40)	

What Is a Rectangle?

Copy below the questions that were raised during
your class discussion about what a rectangle is.

_____

_____

_____

_____

_____

_____

_____

Look in a book or ask someone at home to define a
rectangle, and write that definition on the other side
of this sheet. Try to answer the questions you copied
above with the help of the book or person.

Folding Lines

Make a dotted line on each shape to show where you could fold it so that the two halves fit exactly together. Some shapes will have more than one folding line. Some shapes will have no folding lines. Cut out each shape, and fold it along your line to check it.

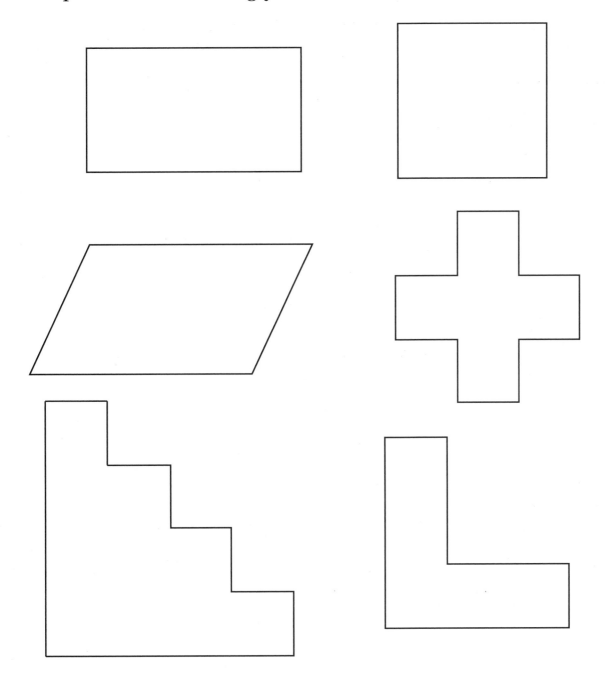

Drawing Symmetrical Patterns (page 1 of 2)

Draw the shape that appears in one quadrant in the other three quadrants to make a symmetrical bulletin board. The heavy lines are the axes. You can fold on these lines to help you see where the shapes need to go to be symmetrical.

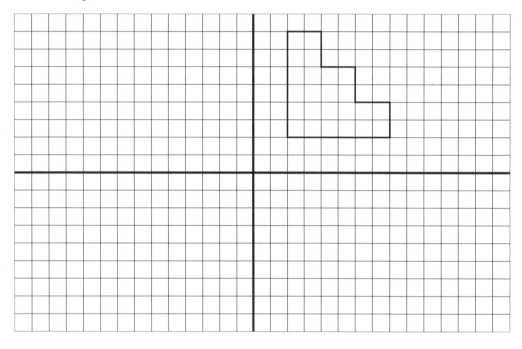

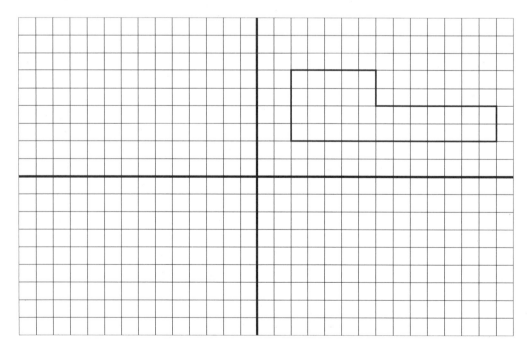

Drawing Symmetrical Patterns (page 2 of 2)

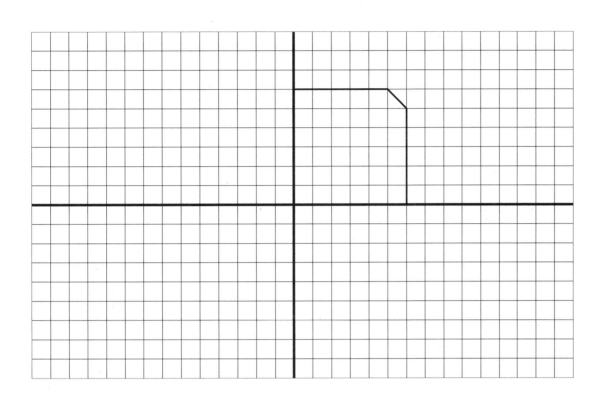

Special Challenge

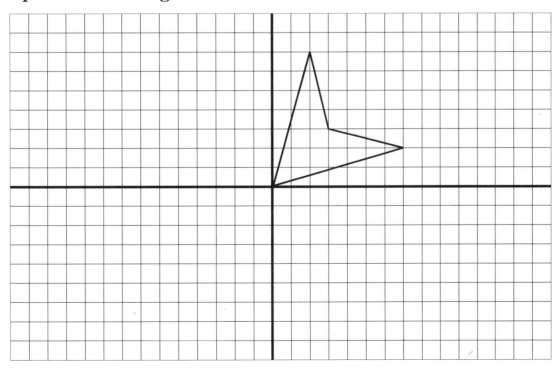

Name Date

Student Sheet 21

Symmetry in the World

Look for pictures that show examples of symmetry in the world. Bring in one or more pictures to post on a symmetry bulletin board on the classroom wall. If you can't find pictures in magazines or newspapers, draw a picture below of something around your house that has symmetry.

Drawing More Symmetrical
Patterns (page 1 of 2)

Draw the shape that appears in one quadrant in the
other three quadrants to make a symmetrical bulletin
board. The heavy lines are the axes. You can fold on
these lines to help you see where the shapes need to
go to be symmetrical.

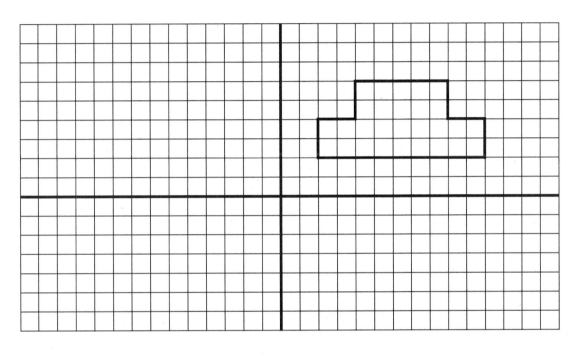

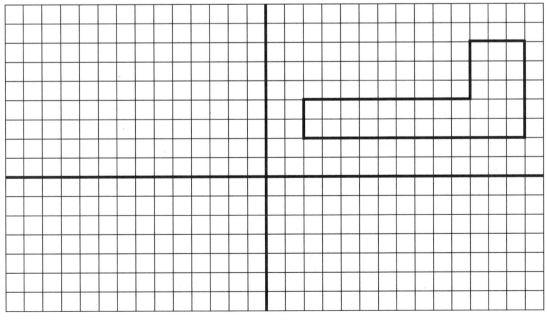

Drawing More Symmetrical
Patterns (page 2 of 2)

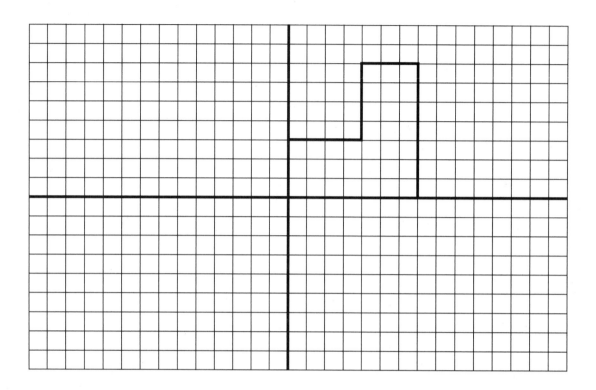

Special Challenge

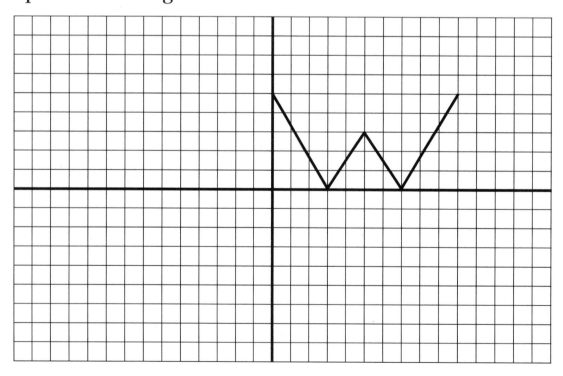

Planning Grid Pictures

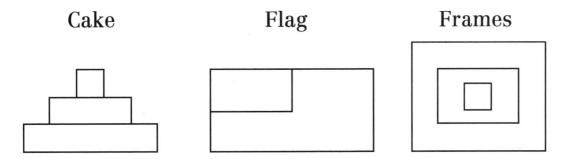

Cake   Flag   Frames

1. Draw each picture on one grid on a piece of Procedure Planning Paper. Draw one picture in Quadrant I, one in Quadrant II, and one partly in Quadrant III and partly in Quadrant IV. Make the pictures any size, but do not overlap them. Write *Geo-Logo* commands to draw each picture. Use only `jumpto` and `rect` commands.

2. Draw your grid pictures on the computer.

   a. Open the Rectangle Pictures activity.

   b. Click the **Grid tool** ▦ to see the grid.

   c. Type each procedure on the computer in the Rectangle Pictures activity.

   d. After entering each procedure, teach it to the computer.

   e. Write a procedure that draws all the shapes on the screen in the quadrants as described above.

Name Date

Student Sheet 24

Analyzing Rectangle Procedures

Look at each of the procedures below. Which procedures would draw rectangles? If a procedure does not draw a rectangle, change it so it does by changing the commands that are shown. Fill in the inputs to the `rect` procedure that would draw the same rectangle. One way to do the first procedure is shown here.

1. Example	**2.**	**3.**
fd 57 rt 90 fd 83 rt 90 ~~fd 67~~ fd 57 rt 90 fd 73 } fd 83 fd 10 } rt 90 rect 57 83	fd 75 rt 90 fd 65 rt 90 fd 20 fd 20 rt 90 fd 50 fd 15 rt 90 rect ___ ___	fd 40 rt 40 rt 40 fd 82 rt 80 fd 40 rt 80 fd 82 rt 90 rect ___ ___
4.	**5.**	**6.**
fd 50 fd 40 rt 90 fd 90 rt 90 fd 90 rt 90 fd 73 fd 17 rt 90 rect ___ ___	fd 70 rt 90 fd 65 rt 90 fd 65 rt 90 fd 50 fd 20 rt 90 rect ___ ___	fd 40 rt 90 fd 55 rt 80 fd 40 rt 80 rt 10 fd 55 rt 90 rect ___ ___

Exploring Turns and Repeats with Rectangles

Do this exploring on the computer in the Rectangle Pictures activity. Use this command:

repeat _____ [rt _____ rect _____ _____]

1. Decide on a rectangle size. Fill in the blanks above.

2. Decide on the size of turn (30, 45, 60, 90, and so on). Fill in the blank. (If you wish, change rt to lt.)

3. Use repeat 1 and run the command.

   Change the command to repeat 2 and run the command.

   Run the command using repeat 3, repeat 4, and repeat 5.

   Predict what will happen when you change the command to repeat 6. Then do repeat 6 on the computer. Did what happened match your prediction? Why or why not?

4. Find a repeat number to make your rectangle go exactly all the way around. Record your command here:

   Change the turn size (and if you wish, your rectangle), and see what happens as you try repeats of 1, 2, 3, 4, 5, and 6.

   Record any commands that you find that turn your rectangle exactly all the way around.

Am I a Rectangle? (page 1 of 2)

Which figures are rectangles? If a figure **is** a rectangle, write the *Geo-Logo* commands you would use to draw it. Use the `rect` procedure with two inputs. You may have to use a turn command for some figures. If the figure is **not** a rectangle, explain why it is not.

1.

_____

_____

_____

2.

_____

_____

_____

3.

_____

_____

_____

4.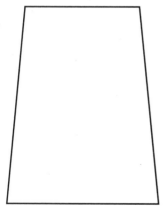

_____

_____

_____

5.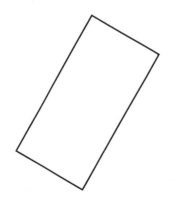

_____

_____

_____

6.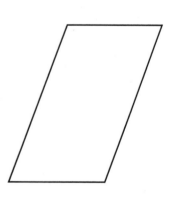

_____

_____

_____

Am I a Rectangle? (page 2 of 2)

7.

8.

9.

_____

_____

_____

10.

11.

12.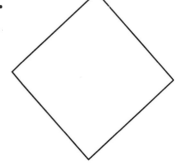

_____

_____

_____

Drawing Rectangle Patterns

Choose one of the Rectangle Patterns procedures below.

Following the commands below, draw the pattern on Procedure Planning Paper. Check your result by entering the procedure on the computer.

```
rect 10 20
rect 20 30
rect 30 40
rect 40 50
rect 50 60
rect 60 70
rect 70 80
rect 80 90
rect 90 100
rect 100 110
```

Teach this procedure to the computer, giving it the name: rects1

What do you think will happen if you now write the following command. Draw it. Try it on the computer.

```
repeat 4 [rects1 rt 90]
```

Following the commands below, draw the pattern on Procedure Planning Paper. Check your result by entering the procedure on the computer.

```
rect 10 100
rect 20 90
rect 30 80
rect 40 70
rect 50 60
rect 60 50
rect 70 40
rect 80 30
rect 90 20
rect 100 10
```

Teach this procedure to the computer, giving it the name: rects2

What do you think will happen if you now write the following command. Draw it. Try it on the computer.

```
repeat 4 [rects2 rt 90]
```

Grids on Real Maps

Many maps are printed with a grid for purposes of measurement and location (for example, lines of longitude and latitude) or location only (for example, rows and columns identified by numbers and letters). Find at least one example of such a map. Look at it carefully so you can explain in class how the grid works.

If you do not have a map with a grid at home, draw a map of a room in your house, draw a grid on it, place the furniture on the grid, then make a "key" to show the location of each piece of furniture. For example, you might say that the sofa is at 3, 4.

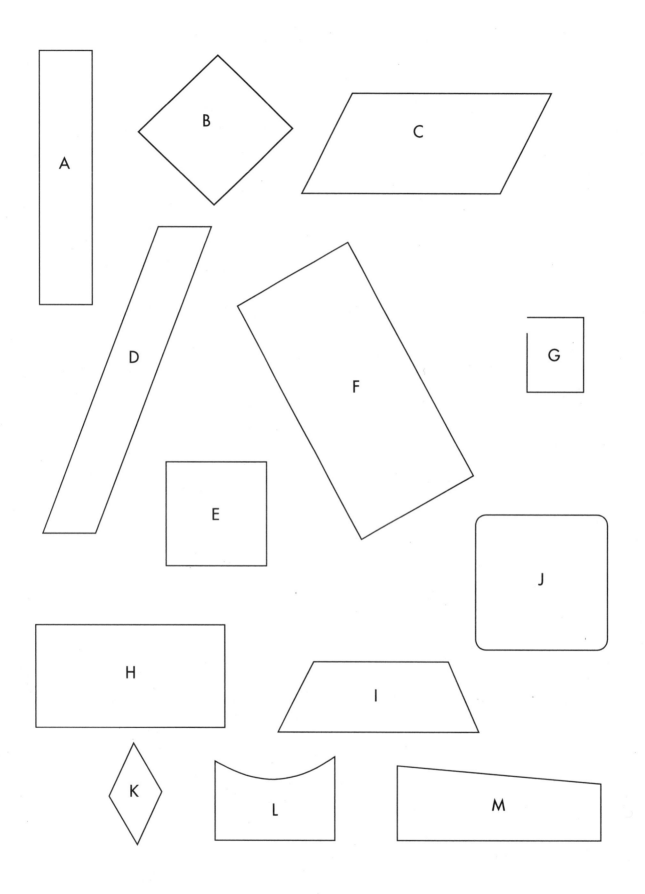

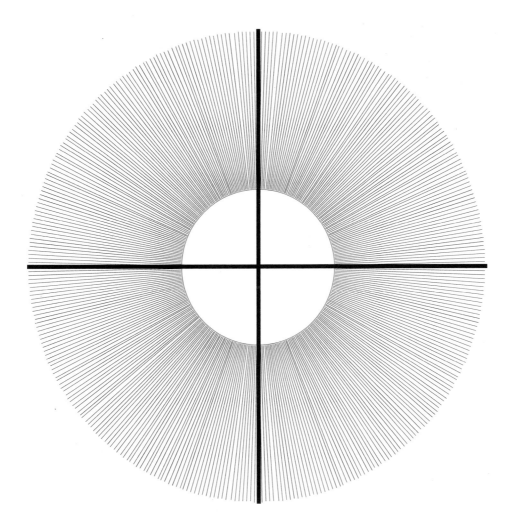

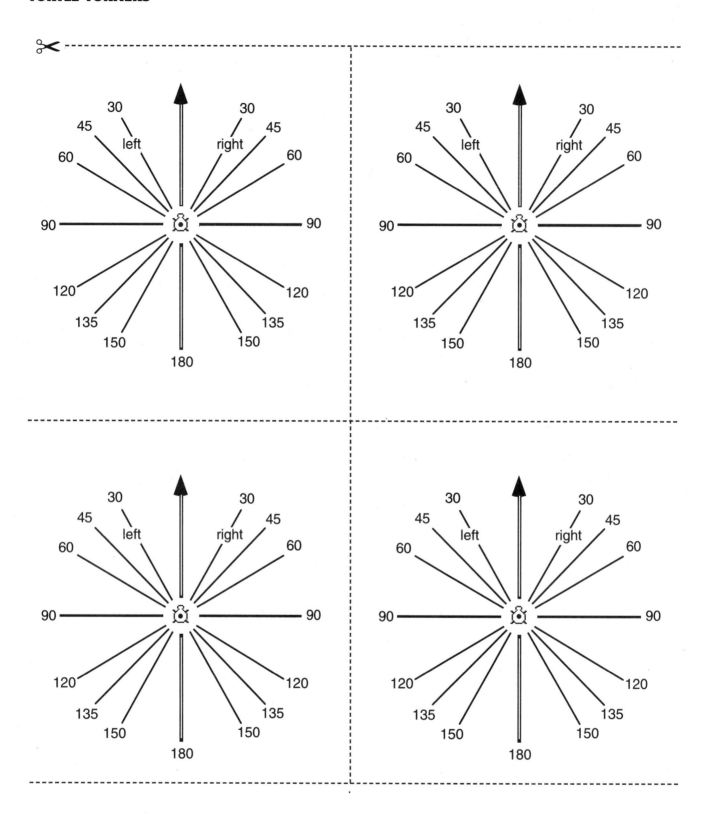

Practice Pages

This optional section provides homework ideas for teachers who want or need to give more homework than is assigned to accompany the activities in this unit. The problems included here provide additional practice in learning about number relationships and in solving computation and number problems. For number units, you may want to use some of these if your students need more work in these areas or if you want to assign daily homework. For other units, you can use these problems so that students can continue to work on developing number and computation sense while they are focusing on other mathematical content in class. We recommend that you introduce activities in class before assigning related problems for homework.

Close to 100 This game is introduced in the unit *Mathematical Thinking at Grade 4*. If your students are familiar with the game, you can simply send home the directions, score sheet, and Numeral Cards so that students can play at home. If your students have not played the game before, introduce it in class and have students play once or twice before sending it home. For more challenge, students can try one of the variations listed at the bottom of the sheet. You might have students do this activity two times for homework in this unit.

Story Problems Story problems at various levels of difficulty are used throughout the *Investigations* curriculum. The three story problem sheets provided here help students review and maintain skills that have already been taught. You can also make up other problems in this format, using numbers and contexts that are appropriate for your students. Students solve the problems and then record their strategies.

Froggy Races This type of problem is introduced in the unit *Landmarks in the Thousands*. Here, you are provided three problem sheets and one 300 chart, which you can copy for use with problem sheets. You can also make up other problems in this format, using numbers that are appropriate for your students. On each sheet, students solve the problems and record their solution strategies.

Materials
- One deck of Numeral Cards
- Close to 100 Score Sheet for each player

Players: 1, 2, or 3

How to Play
1. Deal out six Numeral Cards to each player.
2. Use any four of your cards to make two numbers. For example, a 6 and a 5 could make either 56 or 65. Wild Cards can be used as any numeral. Try to make numbers that, when added, give you a total that is close to 100.
3. Write these two numbers and their total on the Close to 100 Score Sheet. For example: 42 + 56 = 98.
4. Find your score. Your score is the difference between your total and 100. For example, if your total is 98, your score is 2. If your total is 105, your score is 5.
5. Put the cards you used in a discard pile. Keep the two cards you didn't use for the next round.
6. For the next round, deal four new cards to each player. Make more numbers that come close to 100. When you run out of cards, mix up the discard pile and use them again.
7. Five rounds make one game. Total your scores for the five rounds. LOWEST score wins!

Scoring Variation
Write the score with plus and minus signs to show the direction of your total away from 100. For example: If your total is 98, your score is –2. If your total is 105, your score is +5. The total of these two scores would be +3. Your goal is to get a total score for five rounds that is close to 0.

Close to 100 Score Sheet

Name_____

Game 1   Score

Round 1: _____ + _____ = _____   _____

Round 2: _____ + _____ = _____   _____

Round 3: _____ + _____ = _____   _____

Round 4: _____ + _____ = _____   _____

Round 5: _____ + _____ = _____   _____

                                          TOTAL SCORE   _____

Name_____

Game 2   Score

Round 1: _____ + _____ = _____   _____

Round 2: _____ + _____ = _____   _____

Round 3: _____ + _____ = _____   _____

Round 4: _____ + _____ = _____   _____

Round 5: _____ + _____ = _____   _____

                                          TOTAL SCORE   _____

                Sunken Ships and Grid Patterns

0	0	1	1
0	0	1	1
2	2	3	3
2	2	3	3

Practice Page
Sunken Ships and Grid Patterns

4	4	5	5
4	4	5	5
<u>6</u>	<u>6</u>	7	7
<u>6</u>	<u>6</u>	7	7

Practice Page
Sunken Ships and Grid Patterns

8	8	<u>9</u>	<u>9</u>
8	8	<u>9</u>	<u>9</u>

WILD CARD	**WILD CARD**
WILD CARD	**WILD CARD**

176

Practice Page A

For each problem, show how you found your solution.

1. My mom is planning her shopping for the next
    28 days. She buys juice in 9-packs. If my brother
    and I each drink a juice every day, how many
    9-packs will my mom need to buy?

2. My mom will also buy fruit cups. They come in
    6-packs. I don't like them, but my brother does.
    How many 6-packs will she need to buy if he eats
    one every day?

3. We each eat a sandwich every day. Each loaf of
    bread has 30 slices. How many loaves of bread
    should my mom buy?

Practice Page B

For each problem, show how you found your solution.

1. My teacher has a box of 180 tissues. Each of the 25 students in the class used 4 tissues last week. Does my teacher have any tissues left over? If so, how many?

2. This week, each student has used 3 tissues. Does my teacher still have any tissues left in her box? If so, how many?

3. One day last month, every student in my class of 25 had a cold, so each of us used 7 tissues that day. How many tissues was that altogether?

Practice Page C

For each problem, show how you found your solution.

1. There are 78 people at the movie theater. The chairs are set up in rows of 8. How many rows are filled?

2. There are 78 people going on a field trip. They will travel by van. If 8 people fit in each van, how many vans will be needed?

3. Eight people donated 78 dollars altogether to the local homeless shelter. If they each contributed the same amount of money, how much did each one contribute?

300 CHART

1	2	3	4	5	6	7	8	9	10
11	12	13	14	15	16	17	18	19	20
21	22	23	24	25	26	27	28	29	30
31	32	33	34	35	36	37	38	39	40
41	42	43	44	45	46	47	48	49	50
51	52	53	54	55	56	57	58	59	60
61	62	63	64	65	66	67	68	69	70
71	72	73	74	75	76	77	78	79	80
81	82	83	84	85	86	87	88	89	90
91	92	93	94	95	96	97	98	99	100
101	102	103	104	105	106	107	108	109	110
111	112	113	114	115	116	117	118	119	120
121	122	123	124	125	126	127	128	129	130
131	132	133	134	135	136	137	138	139	140
141	142	143	144	145	146	147	148	149	150
151	152	153	154	155	156	157	158	159	160
161	162	163	164	165	166	167	168	169	170
171	172	173	174	175	176	177	178	179	180
181	182	183	184	185	186	187	188	189	190
191	192	193	194	195	196	197	198	199	200
201	202	203	204	205	206	207	208	209	210
211	212	213	214	215	216	217	218	219	220
221	222	223	224	225	226	227	228	229	230
231	232	233	234	235	236	237	238	239	240
241	242	243	244	245	246	247	248	249	250
251	252	253	254	255	256	257	258	259	260
261	262	263	264	265	266	267	268	269	270
271	272	273	274	275	276	277	278	279	280
281	282	283	284	285	286	287	288	289	290
291	292	293	294	295	296	297	298	299	300

Practice Page
Sunken Ships and Grid Patterns

Practice Page D

Solve each problem. You may want to use a 300 Chart to help.

1. Two frogs had a race. Hoppy Frog took 10 jumps of 28. Hurry Frog took 5 jumps of 55. Who was ahead? How do you know?

2. In a second race, Hoppy took 9 jumps of 30. Hurry took 7 jumps of 38. Who was ahead? How do you know?

3. In the last race, Hoppy decided to take jumps of 150. She took 1 jump of 150. How many more jumps of 150 did she need to reach 300? How do you know?

181

Practice Page E

Solve each problem. You may want to use a 300 Chart to help.

1. Two frogs had a race. Iggy Frog took 25 jumps of 7. Itty Frog took 30 jumps of 6. Who was ahead? How do you know?

2. In a second race, Iggy took 7 jumps of 30. Itty took 8 jumps of 26. Who was ahead? How do you know?

3. In the last race, Itty decided to take jumps of 5. He took 26 jumps of 5. How many more jumps of 5 did he need to reach 300? How do you know?

Practice Page F

Solve each problem.

1. Three frogs had a race on an imaginary 1000 chart. Nester Frog took 35 jumps of 25. Number Frog took 35 jumps of 20, and Nooler Frog took 100 jumps of 7. Who was ahead? How do you know?

2. Remember that Nester has taken 35 jumps of 25. How many more jumps of 25 does Nester need to reach 1000? How do you know?